THIS BOOK WAS given to me on FEB 1, 2001
by the members of the Union City
Bergen Ave Hispanic Mosque

١١٠ أحاديث قدسية

110

Ahadith Qudsi

Sayings of the Prophet ﷺ Having Allâhs Statements

Second Edition: July 2003

© Maktaba Dar-us-Salam, 1996

King Fahd National Library Cataloging-in-Publication Data

Masood-ul-Hasan, Sayed

110 Ahadith qudsi-Riyadh.

128p., 14x21 cm.

ISBN 9960-740-84-6

I-Al-Hadith Al-Qudsi II-Title

237.98 dc. 0369/17

Legal Deposit no. 0369/17

ISBN 9960-740-84-6

Head Office: P.O. Box: 22743, Riyadh 11416, K.S.A. Tel: 00966-01-4033962/4043432 Fax: 4021659
E-mail: darussalam@awalnet.net.sa Website: http// www.dar-us-salam.com

K.S.A. Darussalam Showrooms:

Riyadh

Olaya branch: Tel 00966-1-4614483 Fax: 4644945

Malaz branch: Tel 4735220 Fax: 4735221

- **Jeddah**
  Tel: 00966-2-6879254 Fax: 6336270
- **Al-Khobar**
  Tel: 00966-3-8692900 Fax: 00966-3-8691551

U.A.E

- Darussalam, Sharjah U.A.E
  Tel: 00971-6-5632623 Fax: 5632624

PAKISTAN

- Darussalam, 36 B Lower Mall, Lahore
  Tel: 0092-42-724 0024 Fax: 7354072
- Rahman Market, Ghazni Street
  Urdu Bazar Lahore
  Tel: 0092-42-7120054 Fax: 7320703

U.S.A

- Darussalam, Houston
  P.O Box: 79194 Tx 772779
  Tel: 001-713-722 0419 Fax: 001-713-722 0431
  E-mail: sales@dar-us-salam.com
- Darussalam, New York
  572 Atlantic Ave, Brooklyn
  New York-11217, Tel: 001-718-625 5925

U.K

- Darussalam International Publications Ltd.
  226 High Street, Walthamstow,
  London E17 7JH, Tel: 0044-208 520 2666
  Mobile: 0044-794 730 6706 Fax: 0044-208 521 7645
- Darussalam International Publications Limited
  Regent Park Mosque, 146 Park Road,
  London NW8 7RG Tel: 0044-207 724 3363
- Darussalam
  398-400 Coventry Road, Small Heath
  Birmingham, B10 0UF
  Tel: 0121 77204792 Fax: 0121 772 4345
  E-mail: info@darussalamuk.com
  Web: www.darussalamuk.com

FRANCE

- Editions & Librairie Essalam
  135, Bd de Ménilmontant- 75011 Paris
  Tél: 0033-01- 43 38 19 56/ 44 83
  Fax: 0033-01- 43 57 44 31
  E-mail: essalam@essalam.com

AUSTRALIA

- ICIS: Ground Floor 165-171, Haldon St.
  Lakemba NSW 2195, Australia
  Tel: 00612 9758 4040 Fax: 9758 4030

MALAYSIA

- E&D Books SDN. BHD.-321 B 3rd Floor,
  Suria Klcc
  Kuala Lumpur City Center 50088
  Tel: 00603-21663433 Fax: 459 72032

SINGAPORE

- Muslim Converts Association of Singapore
  32 Onan Road The Galaxy Singapore- 424484
  Tel: 0065-440 6924, 348 8344 Fax: 440 6724

SRI LANKA

- Darul Kitab 6, Nimal Road, Colombo-4
  Tel: 0094-1-589 038 Fax: 0094-74 722433

KUWAIT

- Islam Presentation Committee
  Enlightment Book Shop
  P.O. Box: 1613, Safat 13017 Kuwait
  Tel: 00965-244 7526, Fax: 240 0057

INDIA

- Islamic Dimensions
  56/58 Tandel Street (North)
  Dongri, Mumbai 4000 009, India
  Tel: 0091-22-3736875, Fax: 3730689
  E-mail:sales@IRF.net

SOUTH AFRICA

- Islamic Da`wah Movement (IDM)
  48009 Qualbert 4078 Durban, South Africa
  Tel: 0027-31-304-6883
  Fax: 0027-31-305-1292
  E-mail: idm@ion.co.za

١١٠ أحاديث قدسية

110 AHADITH QUDSI

Sayings of the Prophet ﷺ Having Allâhs Statements

Translated by
Syed Masood-ul-Hasan

Revised and Commentaries by
Ibrahim M. Kunna

DARUSSALAM
GLOBAL LEADER IN ISLAMIC BOOKS
Riyadh • Jeddah • Al-Khobar • Sharjah
Lahore • London • Houston • New York

بسم الله الرحمن الرحيم

CONTENTS

بسم الله الرحمن الرحيم

In the Name of Allah, the Most
Beneficent, the Most Merciful

Publishers Note

The main source of Islamic *Shari'ah* is Qur'ân which is revealed in the exact Words of Allâh عزوجل hence it is termed as *Wahy Matlu* (Oft-recited Revelation in Allâh's Words). Qur'ân covers the Divine orders, guiding principles and other facts in a general form. The second source is *Hadith* which are the Traditions of the Prophet صلى الله عليه وسلم. *Ahadith* inform us about the practical aspects of Divine commandments for human life and provide explanations and demonstrations of the basic principles outlined by Allâh عزوجل .

In fact *Ahadith* are the sayings, deeds and approvals of the Prophet صلى الله عليه وسلم under Divine guidance, so these are termed as *Wahy Ghair Matlu* or *Wahy Marvi* (Revelation narrated in the words of the Prophet صلى الله عليه وسلم). Thus *Ahadith* are an indispensable to a Muslim as the Qur'ân is to understand Islam and act according to it.

Some *Ahadith* hold a distinct place and are termed as *Ahadith Qudsi* (Sacred Traditions). Generally *Ahadith* are traced back to the Prophet صلى الله عليه وسلم as regards their authority, but the authority in *Ahadith Qudsi* is attributed to Allâh عزوجل through the Prophet صلى الله عليه وسلم. The distinction between the Qur'ân and *Ahadith Qudsi* is that the Qur'ân is in the direct wording of Allâh as from *Al-Lauh Al-Mahfuz* (the Preserved Tablet) while *Ahadith Qudsi* are from Allâh as to the meaning and from the Prophet as to the wording.

We are producing here a collection of *Ahadith Qudsi* relating to the important aspects of daily life so that the readers may get benefited from it for the success in this life as well as in Hereafter. Original text of the *Ahadith* in the Arabic language is also given with the English translation because the translations do not convey the full meanings of the original language.

May mercy and blessings of Allâh be upon our Prophet Muhammad, his family, Companions and all who follow him.

Abdul-Malik Mujahid
General Manager

بِسْمِ اللَّهِ الرَّحْمَٰنِ الرَّحِيمِ

(١) عنْ أَبِي ذَرٍّ رَضِيَ اللهُ عَنْهُ قال: «قَالَ رَسُوْلُ اللهِ ﷺ: يَقُوْلُ اللهُ عَزَّ وَجَلَّ: مَنْ جَاءَ بِالْحَسَنَةِ فَلَهُ عَشْرُ أَمْثَالِهَا وَأَزِيْدُ، وَمَنْ جَاءَ بِالسَّيِّئَةِ فَجَزَاؤُهُ سَيِّئَةٌ مِثْلُهَا أَوْ أَغْفِرُ وَمَنْ تَقَرَّبَ مِنِّي شِبْرًا تَقَرَّبْتُ مِنْهُ ذِرَاعًا، وَمَنْ تَقَرَّبَ مِنِّي ذِرَاعًا تَقَرَّبْتُ مِنْهُ بَاعًا وَمَنْ أَتَانِي يَمْشِي أَتَيْتُهُ هَرْوَلَةً، وَمَنْ لَقِيَنِي بِقُرَابِ الأَرْضِ خَطِيْئَةً لاَيُشْرِكُ بِي شَيْئًا لَقِيْتُهُ بِمِثْلِهَا مَغْفِرَةً.» «حديث صحيح»

[رواه مسلم وابن ماجة ومسند أحمد]

Superiority of Monotheism

1) Narrated Abû Dhar رضى الله عنه: Allâh's Messenger صلى الله عليه وسلم said that Allâh عز وجل said: He who comes with a good deed, its reward will be ten like that or even more. And he who comes with vice, his reward will be only one like that, or I can forgive him. He who draws close to Me a hand's span, I will draw close to him an arm's length. And whoever draws near Me an arm's length, I will draw near him a fathom's length. And whoever comes to Me walking, I will go to him running. And whoever faces Me with sins nearly as great as the earth, I will meet him with forgiveness nearly as great as that, provided he does not worship something with me.

(This *Hadîth* is sound and reported by Muslim, Ibn Mâjah and Ahmad in his *Musnad*).

Another prophetic tradition says: (He who met Allah associating anything with Him, will enter Hell) (Muslim)

****

(٢) عنْ أَبي سَعِيدٍ الخُدْرِيِّ رَضِيَ اللهُ عَنْهُ قَالَ: قَالَ رَسُولُ اللهِ ﷺ: «مَا مُجادَلَةُ أَحدِكُمْ فِي الحَقِّ يَكُونُ لَهُ فِي الدُّنْيَا بأَشَدَّ مُجَادَلَةً مِنَ المُؤْمِنِيْنَ لِرَبِّهِمْ فِي إِخْوَانِهِمُ الَّذِيْنَ أُدْخِلُوا النَّارَ قَالَ: يَقُولُونَ رَبَّنَا إِخْوَانُنَا كَانُوْا يُصَلُّونَ مَعَنَا وَيَصُومُونَ مَعَنَا وَيَحُجُّونَ مَعَنَا فَأَدْخَلْتَهُمُ النَّارَ؟! قَالَ فَيَقُولُ اذْهَبُوا فَأَخْرِجُوا مَنْ عَرَفْتُمْ مِنْهُمْ. قَالَ فَيَأْتُونَهُمْ فَيَعْرِفُوْنَهُمْ بِصُوَرِهِمْ فَمِنْهُمْ مَنْ أَخَذَتْهُ النَّارُ إِلَى أَنْصَافِ سَاقَيْهِ، وَمِنْهُمْ مَنْ أَخَذَتْهُ إِلَى كَعْبَيْهِ فَيُخْرِجُوْنَهُمْ فَيَقُولُوْنَ رَبَّنَا قَدْ أَخْرجنَا مَنْ أَمَرْتَنَا. قَالَ وَيَقُولُ: أَخْرِجُوا مَنْ كَانَ فِي قَلْبِهِ وَزْنُ دِيْنَارٍ مِنَ الإِيْمَانِ، ثُمَّ قَالَ: مَنْ كَانَ فِي قَلْبِهِ وَزْنُ نِصْفِ دِيْنَارٍ حَتَّى يَقُوْلَ مَنْ كَانَ فِي قَلْبِهِ وَزْنُ ذَرَّةٍ» «حديث صحيح» [رواه النسائي وابن ماجه].

قَالَ أَبُو سَعِيْدٍ: مَنْ لَمْ يُصَدِّقْ فَلْيَقْرَأْ هَذِهِ الآيَةَ ﴿إِنَّ اللهَ لاَ يَغْفِرُ أَنْ يُشْرَكَ بِهِ وَيَغْفِرُ مَا دُوْنَ ذَلِكَ لِمَنْ يَشَاءُ إِلَى . . . عَظِيْمًا﴾.

2) Narrated Abû Sa'îd Al-Khudri رضى الله عنه: Allâh's Messenger صلى الله عليه وسلم said: None of you will have argued for his right in the world more vehemently than the believers who will do with their Lord about their brethren who were admitted into Hell. The Prophet صلى الله عليه وسلم added: They will say: O Lord! Our brethren used to offer prayers with us, observe fast with us and perform pilgrimage (*Hajj*) with us. But You cast them into fire. The

Prophet صلى الله عليه وسلم further said: Allâh will say: Go and bring out whoever you know from among them. The Prophet صلى الله عليه وسلم said: The believers will come to them and recognize them by face. Some of them will be those the fire would have seized up to half of their shanks and some of them up to their ankles. They will bring them and say: O Lord! We have taken out those for whom you gave us order. Then the Prophet صلى الله عليه وسلم said: Allâh will say: Bring out whoever has in his heart any belief weighing a Dinâr (a coin). Then He will say: Take out whoever has in his heart the belief weighing half a Dinâr until He will say: Take out whoever has in his heart the belief that equals the weight of an atom.

(This *Hadîth* is sound and reported by Nasa'i and Ibn Mâjah).

After narrating this *Hadîth*, Abû Sa'îd said: He who does not accept it as true should read this verse:

(ان الله لا يغفر أن يشرك به و يغفر ما دون ذلك لمن يشاء ... حتى... عظيما)

"Verily, Allâh forgives not that partners should be set up with Him in worship, but He forgives except that (anything else) to whom He pleases, and whoever sets up partners with Allâh in worship, he has indeed invented a tremendous sin." (4:48)

****

(٣) عَنْ أَبِي هُرَيرَةَ رَضِيَ اللهُ عَنْهُ عَنِ النَّبِيِّ ﷺ قَالَ: «يَلْقَى إِبْرَاهِيْمُ أَبَاهُ آزَرَ يَوْمَ الْقِيَامَةِ وَعَلَى وَجْهِ آزَرَ قَتَرَةٌ وَغَبَرَةٌ فَيَقُوْلُ لَهُ إِبْرَاهِيْمُ أَبَاهُ آزَرَ يَوْمَ الْقِيَامَةِ وَعَلَى وَجْهِ آزَرَ قَتَرَةٌ وَغَبَرَةٌ فَيَقُوْلُ لَهُ إِبْرَاهِيْمُ: أَلَمْ أَقُلْ لَكَ لَاتَعْصِنِي؟ فَيَقُوْلُ أَبُوْهُ: فَالْيَوْمَ لَاأَعْصِيكَ فَيَقُوْلُ إِبْرَاهِيْمُ: يَارَبِّ إِنَّكَ وَعَدْتَنِي أَنْ لَاتُخْزِيْنِي يَوْمَ يُبْعَثُوْنَ، فَأَيُّ خِزْيٍ أَخْزَى مِنْ أَبِي الأَبْعَدِ فَيَقُوْلُ اللهُ

تَعَالَى : إِنِّي حَرَّمْتُ الْجَنَّةَ عَلَى الْكَافِرِيْنَ ثُمَّ يُقَالُ يَا إِبْرَاهِيْمُ مَا تَحْتَ رِجْلَيْكَ؟ ! ! فَيَنْظُرُ فَإِذَا هُوَ بِذِيْخٍ مُلْتَطِخٍ فَيُؤْخَذُ بِقَوَائِمِهِ فَيُلْقَى فِي النَّارِ» . «حديث صحيح» [رواه البخاري]

Hazardousness of *Shirk* (joining partners with Allâh)

3) Narrated Abû Huraira رضى الله عنه that Prophet Muhammad صلى الله عليه وسلم said: On the Day of Resurrection, Ibrâhim (Abraham) will see his father Azar (in such a pitiable condition) that his face will be dark and covered with dust. Then Ibrâhim will remind him: Did I not warn you against denying me? His father will reply: Today I will not deny you. Then, Ibrâhim will say: O Lord! You have promised not to disgrace me on the Day of Resurrection. So what will be more disgraceful to me than my wretched father. Allâh تبارك و تعالى will say: I have forbidden Paradise for disbelievers. Then it will be said: O Ibrâhim, Look! what is underneath your feet? He will look and see his father as a Hyena — besmeared with dirt caught by the legs and thrown into Hell.

Due to infidelity, Azar will not be forgiven inspite of his son Ibrahim's intercession for him and he will be transformed into an animal and cast into Hell. It also proves that the pagans whoever they are by kinship, will be forbidden from entering Paradise for ever. They will remain in Hell and suffer the agonies of torment which they had been frightened of by the Messengers of Allah at different times.

****

(٤) عَنْ أَنَسِ بْنِ مَالِكٍ رَضِيَ اللهُ عَنْهُ عَنِ النَّبِيِّ ﷺ قَالَ : يَقُولُ اللهُ تَعَالَى لأَهْوَنَ أَهْلِ النَّارِ عَذَابًا يومَ القِيَامَةِ : «لَوْ أَنَّ لَكَ مَا فِي الأَرْضِ مِنْ شَيْءٍ أَكُنْتَ تَفْتَدِيْ بِهِ؟ فَيَقُولُ نَعَمْ فَيَقُوْلُ أَرَدْتُ مِنْكَ أَهْوَنَ مِنْ هَذَا وَأَنْتَ فِي صُلْبِ آدَمَ : أَنْ

لاَتُشْرِكْ بِي شَيْئًا فَأَبَيْتَ إِلاَّ أَنْ تُشْرِكَ بِي . «حديث صحيح »

[رواه البخاري ومسلم]

4) Narrated Anas bin Mâlik رضى الله عنه on the authority of the Prophet صلى الله عليه وسلم, who said: Allâh تبارك و تعالى will say to the least tormented person among the people of Hell on the Day of Resurrection: Do you have any thing on earth, that you would give as a ransom (to protect yourself against the torment of Fire)? He will say: Yes. Then Allâh will say: While you were in the backbone of Adam, I had demanded you much less than that, i.e. to associate nothing with Me; but you declined and worshipped others besides Me.

(This *Hadîth* is sound and reported by Bukhâri and Muslim).

This *Hadith* concludes that a believer with his sins covering the entire globe will be forgiven so long as he does not associate partners to Allah.

****

(٥) عَنْ مَحْمُودِ بْنِ لَبِيْدٍ رَضِيَ اللهُ عَنْهُ قَالَ : قَالَ رَسُولُ اللهِ ﷺ : «إِنَّ أَخْوَفَ مَا أَخَافُ عَلَيْكُمْ الشِّرْكُ الأَصْغَرُ» قَالُوا : وَمَا الشِّرْكُ الأَصْغَرُ يَارَسُوْلَ اللهِ؟ قَالَ : «الرِّيَاءُ» يَقُولُ اللَّهُ عَزَّ وَجَلَّ لَهُمْ يَوْمَ القِيَامَةِ ـ إِذَا جَزَى النَّاسَ بِأَعْمَالِهِمْ ـ: اذْهَبُوْاإِلَى الَّذِيْنَ كُنْتُمْ تُرَاءونَ فِي الدُّنْيَا فَانْظُرُوْا هَلْ تَجِدُوْنَ عِنْدَهُمْ جَزَاءً» . «حديث صحيح» [رواه مسند أحمد]

Warning against hypocrisy

5) Narrated Mahmud bin Labid رضى الله عنه: Allâh's Messenger صلى الله عليه وسلم said: The most dreadful thing

which I fear about you is minor polytheism. The companions asked: What is the minor polytheism? He said: It is hypocrisy; and he added that on the Day of Judgment, when rewarding people for their deeds, Allâh (تبارك و تعالى) will say to the hypocrites: Go to those for the sake of whom you used to perform good deeds; and see whether you can get any reward from them.

(This *Hadîth* is sound and mentioned in *Musnad Ahmad*).

****

(٦) عَنْ أَبِي هُرَيْرَةَ رَضِيَ اللهُ عَنْهُ قَالَ: قَالَ رَسُولُ اللهِ ﷺ «قَالَ اللهُ تَبَارَكَ وَتَعَالَى: أَنَا أَغْنَى الشُّرَكَاءِ عَنِ الشِّرْكِ، مَنْ عَمِلَ عَمَلاً أَشْرَكَ فِيهِ مَعِي غَيْرِي تَرَكْتُهُ وَشِرْكَهُ». «حديث صحيح» [رواه مسلم]

6) Narrated Abû Huraira رضي الله عنه: Allâh's Messenger صلى الله عليه وسلم said: Allâh تبارك و تعالى said: Among all partners, I am the most dispensable with association. So anyone who performs a deed in which he ascribes to Me others; I will abandon him and his act of polytheism.

(This *Hadîth* is sound and reported by Muslim).

Shirk (polytheism) is a sin that if its doer dies without repentance, he will never be forgiven. Verily, whosoever sets up partners in worship with Allah, Allah has forbidden Paradise for him; and the Fire will be his abode.

****

(٧) عَنْ أَبِي هُرَيْرَةَ رَضِيَ اللهُ عَنْهُ قَالَ: سَمِعْتُ رَسُولَ اللهِ ﷺ يَقُولُ: «إِنَّ أَوَّلَ النَّاسِ يُقْضَى يَوْمَ الْقِيَامَةِ عَلَيْهِ رَجُلٌ اسْتُشْهِدَ فَأُتِيَ بِهِ فَعَرَّفَهُ نِعَمَهُ فَعَرَفَهَا قَالَ: فَمَا عَمِلْتَ فِيهَا؟

قَالَ: قَاتَلْتُ فِيكَ حَتَّى اسْتُشْهِدْتُ قَالَ: كَذَبْتَ، وَلَكِنَّكَ قَاتَلْتَ لأَنْ يُقَالَ جَرِيءٌ فَقَدْ قِيْلَ ثُمَّ أُمِرَ بِهِ فَسُحِبَ عَلَى وَجْهِهِ حَتَّى أُلْقِيَ فِي النَّارِ، وَرَجُلٌ تَعَلَّمَ الْعِلْمَ وَعَلَّمَهُ وَقَرَأَ الْقُرْآنَ فَأُتِيَ بِهِ فَعَرَّفَهُ نِعَمَهُ فَعَرَفَهَا قَالَ: فَمَا عَمِلْتَ فِيْهَا؟ قَالَ: تَعَلَّمْتُ العِلْمَ وَعَلَّمْتُهُ وَقَرَأْتُ فِيكَ الْقُرْآنَ قَالَ: كَذَبْتَ وَلَكِنَّكَ تَعَلَّمْتَ لِيُقَالَ عَالِمٌ وَقَرَأْتَ الْقُرْآنَ لِيُقَالَ هُوَ قَارِيءٌ فَقَدْ قِيْلَ. ثُمَّ أُمِرَ بِهِ فَسُحِبَ عَلَى وَجْهِهِ حَتَّى أُلْقِيَ فِي النَّارِ، وَرَجُلٌ وَسَّعَ اللهُ عَلَيْهِ وَأَعْطَاهُ مِنْ أَصْنَافِ الْمَالِ كُلِّهِ فَأُتِيَ بِهِ فَعَرَّفَهُ نِعَمَهُ فَعَرَفَهَا قَالَ: فَمَا عَمِلْتَ فِيْهَا؟ قَالَ: مَا تَرَكْتُ مِنْ سَبِيْلٍ تُحِبُّ أَنْ يُنْفَقَ فِيْهَا إِلاَّ أَنْفَقْتُهُ فِيْهَا لَكَ قَالَ: كَذَبْتَ، وَلَكِنَّكَ فَعَلْتَ لِيُقَالَ هُوَ جَوَادٌ فَقَدْ قِيْلَ ثُمَّ أُمِرَ بِهِ فَسُحِبَ عَلَى وَجْهِهِ ثُمَّ أُلْقِيَ فِي النَّارِ». «حديث صحيح» [رواه مسلم والنسائي]

One whose intention is not pure will deserve Hell. Purity of intention is essential in all deeds

7) Narrated Abû Huraira رضي الله عنه: I heard Allâh's Messenger صلى الله عليه وسلم saying: The first of the people whose case will be decided on the Day of Judgment will be a man who died as a martyr. He will be brought forth. Allâh will make him know about His blessings (which He had bestowed on him in the world). The man will acknowledge them. Then Allâh will ask him: What did you do with them? He will say: I fought in Your way until I died as a martyr. Allâh will remark: You are lying. You

fought so that you may be called a brave warrior. Then orders will be passed against him. So he will be dragged along on his face and cast into Hell.

Second will be a man who studied (religious) knowledge. Then he taught it to others and recited the Qur'ân. He will be brought (for Judgment). Allâh will remind him of His favours (showered on him in the world). He will admit them (having enjoyed them in his life). Then Allâh will ask him: What did you do with them? He will reply: I acquired knowledge and imparted it and also recited the Qur'ân for Your sake. Allâh will observe: You have told a lie, for you got knowledge to be renowned as a scholar; and you recited the Qur'ân to be marked as a *Qâri* (one who recites the Qur'ân according to the rules). Then orders will be passed against him. So he will be dragged along on his face and thrown into Hell.

Third will be a man to whom Allâh had made abundantly rich and granted him every kind of wealth. He will be brought for Judgment. Allâh will let him know about His gifts conferred upon him in the world. He will recognize them. Then Allâh will inquire: What did you with them? He will say: I left no way in which you like money to be spent without spending in it for your sake. Allâh will say: You are lying. You did so to be described as generous (in the society); (It means you got your reward in the world according to your intention). Now you deserve nothing in the Hereafter except Hell). So orders will be passed against him and he will be dragged along on his face until he will be hurled into Hell.

(This *Hadîth* is sound and reported by Muslim and Nasa'i)

The purity of inteniton is behind any deed. If you spend for show, there is no reward. Eventually, if one loves another for something worldly this shall not count in the Hereafter. But love for the sake of Allah عز وجل is great virtue in the Hereafter. Such love can be a Muslim's love to learn from him or to take as a companion for good deeds, without any worldly considerations, once there is something worldly, the intention is not pure.

****

(٨) عَنْ أَبِي مُوسَى رَضِيَ اللهُ عَنْهُ قَالَ: قَالَ رَسُولُ اللهِ ﷺ: «تُحْشَرُ هَذِهِ الأُمَّةُ عَلَى ثَلاثَةِ أَصْنَافٍ: (صِنْفٌ) يَدْخُلُونَ الجَنَّةَ بِغَيْرِ حِسَابٍ، (وَصِنْفٌ) يُحَاسَبُونَ حِسَابًا يَسِيْرًا ثُمَّ يَدْخُلُونَ الجَنَّةَ، (وَصِنْفٌ) يَجِيْئُونَ عَلَى ظُهُوْرِهِمْ أَمْثَالُ الْجِبَالِ الرَّاسِيَاتِ ذُنُوْبًا فَيَسْأَلُ اللَّهُ عَنْهُمْ وَهُوَ أَعْلَمُ بِهِمْ فَيَقُولُ: مَا هَؤُلاَءِ فَيَقُوْلُونَ هَؤُلاَءِ عَبِيْدٌ مِنْ عِبَادِكَ فَيَقُوْلُ حُطُّوْهَا عَنْهُمْ وَاجْعَلُوهَا عَلَى اليَهُوْدِ وَالنَّصَارَى وَأَدْخِلُوْهُمْ بِرَحْمَتِي الجَنَّةَ». «حديث حسن» [رواه مستدرك الحاكم]

Superiority of the believers in the Oneness of Allâh and the punishment of Jews and Christians

8) Narrated Abû Mûsa رضي الله عنه: Allâh's Messenger صلى الله عليه وسلم said: On the Day of Resurrection, my *Ummah* (nation) will be gathered into three groups. one sort will enter Paradise without rendering an account (of their deeds). Another sort will be reckoned an easy account and admitted into Paradise. Yet another sort will come bearing on their backs heaps of sins like great mountains. Allâh will ask the angels though He knows best about them: Who are these people? They will reply: They are humble slaves of yours. He will say: Unload the sins from them

and put the same over the Jews and Christians; then let the humble slaves get into Paradise by virtue of My Mercy.

(This *Hadîth* is sound and mentioned in *Mustadrak* of Hâkim).

****

(٩) عَنِ ابْنِ مَسْعُوْدٍ رَضِيَ اللهُ عَنْهُ أَنَّ النَّبِيَّ ﷺ قال: «عُرِضَتِ الأُمَمُ بِالمَوْسِمِ فَرَأَيْتُ أُمَّتِي فَأَعْجَبَتْنِي كَثْرَتُهُمْ وَهَيْئَتُهُمْ قَدْ مَلأُوْا السَّهَلَ وَالجَبَلَ فَقَالَ: يَامُحَمَّدُ أَرَضِيْتَ؟ قُلْتُ: نَعَمْ أَيْ رَبِّ قَالَ: وَمَعَ هَؤُلاَءِ سَبْعُوْنَ أَلْفًا يَدْخُلُونَ الجَنَّةَ بِغَيْرِ حِسَابٍ الَّذِيْنَ لاَيَسْتَرْقُوْنَ وَلاَ يَكْتَوُوْنَ وَلاَ يَتَطَيَّرُوْنَ وَعَلَى رَبِّهِمْ يَتَوَكَّلُونَ فَقَالَ عُكَّاشَةُ ادْعُ اللهَ أَنْ يَجْعَلَنِيْ مِنْهُمْ فَقَالَ اَللَّهُمَّ اجْعَلْهُ مِنْهُمْ ثُمَّ قَالَ رَجُلٌ آخَرُ: أُدْعُ اللهَ أَنْ يَجْعَلَنِي مِنْهُمْ قَالَ: سَبَقَكَ بِهَا عُكَّاشَةُ». «حديث صحيح»

[موارد الظمآن لزوائد ابن حبان]

Superiority of those who neither treat with amulet, nor get themselves branded nor take omens

9) Narrated Ibn Mas'ûd رضى الله عنه that Prophet Muhammad صلى الله عليه وسلم said: On the Day of Resurrection nations will be brought. When I see my nation (*Ummah*) I will be amazed at their multitudes and (distinguished) form. They will have filled up the plain lands as well as the mountains. Allâh will ask me: Are you satisfied? I will say: Yes, O my Lord: He will say: Along with these

(people), seventy thousand persons (i.e., so many) will enter Paradise without rendering an account. They will be those who neither cure themselves with *Ruqya* (recitations) nor get themselves branded (cauterized), nor take omens but they instead repose trust in their Lord. Upon this, 'Ukkasha said: Supplicate Allâh (that He makes me one among them), the Prophet صلى الله عليه وسلم said: O Allâh! Make him one of them. Another person said: Invoke a blessing for me too (that Allâh makes me one among them). The Prophet صلى الله عليه وسلم said: 'Ukkasha has preceded you in this matter.

(This *Hadîth* is sound and reported by Ibn Hibbân in his book موارد الظمآن لزوائد ابن حبان).

An amulet is something worn around the neck for protection against evil spirits or spell.

****

(١٠) عَنْ أَبِي هُرَيرَةَ رَضِيَ اللهُ عَنْهُ عَنِ النَّبِيِّ ﷺ قَالَ: «قَالَ اللهُ عَزَّ وَجَلَّ: سَبَقَتْ رَحْمَتِي غَضَبِي».

«حديث صحيح» [رواه مسلم]

Broadness of Allâh's Mercy

10) Narrated Abû Huraira رضى الله عنه that Prophet Muhammad صلى الله عليه وسلم who said: Allâh عز وجل said: My mercy has preceded (excelled) my wrath.

(This *Hadîth* is sound and reported by Muslim).

****

(١١) عَنْ أَبِي هُرَيرَةَ رَضِيَ اللهُ عَنْهُ أَنَّ رَسُولَ اللهِ ﷺ قَالَ: «يَقُولُ اللهُ: إِذَا أَرَادَ عَبْدِي أَنْ يَعْمَلَ سَيِّئَةً فَلَا تَكْتُبُوهَا عَلَيْهِ

حَتَّى يَعْمَلَهَا فَإِنْ عَمِلَهَا فَاكْتُبُوهَا بِمِثْلِهَا، وَإِنْ تَرَكَهَا مِنْ أَجْلِي فَاكْتُبُوْهَا لَهُ حَسَنَةً وَإِذَا أَرَادَ أَنْ يَعْمَلَ حَسَنَةً فَلَمْ يَعْمَلْهَا فَاكْتُبُوْهَا لَهُ حَسَنَةً، فَإِنْ عَمِلَهَا فَاكْتُبُوْهَا لَهُ بِعَشْرِ أَمْثَالِهَاإِلَى سَبْعِمِائَةٍ». «حديث صحيح» [رواه البخاري ومسلم والترمذي]

An example of Allâh's Mercy on his slaves

11) Narrated Abû Huraira رضى الله عنه that Allâh's Messenger صلى الله عليه وسلم said: Allâh says: Whenever My slave intends to do a bad deed, (I say to the deeds recording angels): Do not record it against him until he (actually) commits it. If he has done so, write it down exactly as one in his record book. But if he refrains from it for My sake, write down this as a virtue in his favour. And when he intends to do a good deed, but does not actually do it, write it as a virtue for him. And if he puts it into practice, write its reward equal to, from ten to seven hundred times (in his account).

(This *Hadîth* is sound and reported by Bukhâri, Muslim and Tirmidhi).

This above *Hadith* briefly describes that Allah, if He likes, can forgive even the most sinner person believing in Oneness of Allah and the Prophethood of Muhammad صلى الله عليه وسلم. But it doesn't mean that every one should take it as a cover and involve himself intentionally in evils relying on the Mercy of Allah. A good Muslim who has in his heart fear of Allah, should perform righteous deeds and avoid sins as per commands laid down in the Qur'ân and *Hadith.*

****

(١٢) عَنْ أَبِي هُرَيْرَةَ رَضِيَ اللهُ عَنْهُ قَالَ: سَمِعْتُ رَسُولَ اللهِ ﷺ يَقُولُ: «كَانَ رَجُلَانِ فِي بَنِي إِسْرَائِيْلَ مُتَوَاخِيَيْنِ أَحَدُهُمَا يُذْنِبُ وَالآخَرُ مُجْتَهِدٌ فِي العِبَادَةِ فَكَانَ لَايَزَالُ

الْمُجْتَهِدُ يَرَى الآخَرَ عَلَى الذَّنْبِ فَيَقُولُ اقْصُرْ فَوَجَدَهُ يَوْمًا عَلَى ذَنْبٍ فَقَالَ لَهُ: اقْصُرْ فَقَالَ: خَلِّنِي وَرَبِّي أَبُعِثْتَ عَلَيَّ رَقِيبًا فَقَالَ: وَاللهِ لاَ يَغْفِرُ اللهُ لَكَ أَوْ لاَ يُدْخِلُكَ اللهُ الجَنَّةَ فَقَبَضَ أَرْوَاحَهُمَا فَاجْتَمَعَا عِنْدَ رَبِّ العَالَمِينَ فَقَالَ لِهَذَا الْمُجْتَهِدِ: أَكُنْتَ بِي عَالِمًا؟ أَوْ كُنْتَ عَلَى مَا فِي يَدِي قَادِرًا؟ وَقَالَ لِلْمُذْنِبِ: اذْهَبْ فَادْخُلِ الْجَنَّةَ بِرَحْمَتِي وَقَالَ لِلآخَرِ: اذْهَبُوا بِهِ إِلَى النَّارِ». «حديث حسن» [سنن أبي داؤود]

وقَالَ أَبُو هُرَيرَةَ: «وَالَّذِي نَفْسِي بِيَدِهِ لتكَلَّمَ بِكَلِمَةٍ أَوْ بَقَتْ دُنْيَاهُ وَآخِرَتُهُ».

Warning to those who loose hope in the Mercy of Allâh

12) Narrated Abû Huraira رضي الله عنه: I heard Allâh's Messenger صلى الله عليه وسلم saying: There were two fraternal persons among the Children of Israel. One of them was engrossed in committing sins while the other was devoted to worship. The devotee used to see his fellow committing sin and advise him: Desist from doing so. One day when he found his fellow committing sin. He said to him: Avoid it. His fellow said: Leave me alone. Have you been sent out as a vigilant on me. The devotee said: By Allâh, He will neither forgive you nor admit you to Paradise. When they died, they were gathered before the Lord of the worlds. Allâh asked the devotee: Were you assured of knowing Me or were you having power over what was in My Hands? Then He said to the sinner: Go and enter

Paradise by My Mercy; and ordered the angels about the devotee: Lead him to Hell.

(This *Hadîth* is sound and reported by Abû Dâ'ud in his *Sunan*).

After narrating the *Hadîth*, Abû Huraira commented: By Him in Whose Hand my soul is: One word spoken by the devotee ruined his good deeds in the world as well as in the Hereafter.

This *Hadith* signifies that no body should claim whether one would enter Paradise or step into Hell because the verdict here, is for Allah Who is All-Omnipotent over every thing, will decide whatever He likes. A righteous person is required to do good and avoid evil for the sake of Allah only and advise others with the same. He should not say such words as to challenge the authority of Allah. Moreover, it is wrong to feel desperate from the Mercy of Allah.

****

(١٣) عن جندب رضي الله عنه أن رسول الله ﷺ حدث أن رجلا قال: «وَاللهِ لاَيَغْفِرُ اللهُ لِفُلاَنٍ وَأَنَّ اللهَ تَعَالَى قَالَ مَنْ ذَا الَّذِي يَتَأَلَّى عَلَيَّ أَنْ لاَأَغْفِرَ لِفُلاَنٍ فَإِنِّي قَدْ غَفَرْتُ لِفُلاَنٍ وَأَحْبَطْتُ عَمَلَكَ أَوْ كَمَا قَالَ». «حديث صحيح»

[رواه مسلم ومعجم الطبراني الكبير]

13) Narrated Jundub رضي الله عنه that Allâh's Messenger صلى الله عليه وسلم stated that a person said: By Allâh! Allâh will not forgive so-and-so (person). Thereupon Allâh, the Exalted, remarked: Who is he who swears by Me (and says) that I will not forgive so-and-so (listen!) Verily I have forgiven so-and-so and nullified your deeds, or as the Messenger صلى الله عليه وسلم said.

(This *Hadîth* is sound and reported by Muslim and also mentioned in *Mu'jam At-Tabrâni Al-Kabîr*).

This *Hadith* teaches us the politeness needed by a Muslim towards Allah عز وجل and that one should not involve himself in matters that are left for Allah عز وجل to decide i.e. nobody can know who will go to Hell and who will enter Paradise.

****

(١٤) عَنْ أَبِي سَعِيدٍ الْخُدْرِيِّ رَضِيَ اللهُ عَنْهُ عَنِ النَّبِيِّ ﷺ «أَنَّهُ ذَكَرَ رَجُلاً فِيمَا سَلَفَ - أَوْ فِيمَنْ كَانَ قَبْلَكُمْ - قَالَ كَلِمَةً يَعْنِي أَعْطَاهُ مَالاً وَوَلَدًا فَلَمَّا حَضَرَتِ الْوَفَاةُ قَالَ لِبَنِيهِ: أَيَّ أَبٍ كُنْتُ لَكُمْ؟ قَالُوا: خَيْرُ أَبٍ. قَالَ: فَإِنَّهُ لَمْ يَبْتَئِزْ - أَوْ لَمْ يَبْتَئِرْ - عِنْدَ اللهِ خَيْرًا، وَإِنْ يُقَدِّرُ اللهُ عَلَيْهِ يُعَذِّبْهُ فَانْظُرُوا إِذَا مِتُّ فَأَحْرِقُوْنِي حَتَّى إِذَا صِرْتُ فَحْمًا فَاسْحِقُونِي أَوْ قَالَ فَاسْحَكُونِي فَإِذَا كَانَ يَوْمُ رِيحٍ عَاصِفٍ فَأَذْرُوْنِي فِيهَا فَقَالَ نَبِيُّ اللهِ ﷺ: فَأَخَذَ مَوَاثِيقَهُمْ عَلَى ذَلِكَ وَرَبِّي فَفَعَلُوا ثُمَّ أَذْرُوْهُ فِي يَوْمٍ عَاصِفٍ فَقَالَ اللهُ عَزَّ وَجَلَّ: كُنْ فَإِذَا هُوَ رَجُلٌ قَائِمٌ قَالَ اللهُ: أَيْ عَبْدِي مَا حَمَلَكَ عَلَى أَنْ فَعَلْتَ مَا فَعَلْتَ؟ قَالَ: مَخَافَتُكَ - أَوْ فَرَقٌ مِنْكَ - قَالَ: فَمَا تَلَافَاهُ أَنْ رَحِمَهُ عِنْدَهَا، وَقَالَ مَرَّةً أُخْرَى فَمَا تَلَافَاهُ غَيْرُهَا». «حديث صحيح» [رواه البخاري ومسلم]

Fear of Allâh

14) Narrated Abû Sa'îd Al-Khudri رضى الله عنه. He quoted Prophet Muhammad صلى الله عليه وسلم as saying to his Companions that: a man from among the early people or from those before you had said a word, i.e. Allâh had blessed him with wealth and sons. When death approached

him, he asked his sons: How was I being as a father? They replied: You were the best father. He said: I didn't save or perform any good deeds for Allâh. If Allâh takes possession of me, He will punish me. So, look! when I am dead, burn me until I become coal then crush me well and scatter (my ashes in the air) on a stormy day. The Prophet صلى الله عليه وسلم said: He took a covenant from his sons (and died). They did according to his will and spread his ashes in the air on a stormy day. Allâh عز وجل said: Be and there he was embodied before Him. Allâh, the Exalted, asked him: O my slave! what induced you to do what you did. He replied: It was Your fear (so that I may not appear before You). The Prophet صلى الله عليه وسلم added: Allâh, the Exalted rewarded him with His Mercy; the Prophet صلى الله عليه وسلم said second time: Allâh did not punish him.

(This *Hadîth* is sound and reported by Bukhâri and Muslim).

This man was a believer in the Power of Allah عز وجل to resurrect, and punish. His such belief and fear caused him to make that will which led him to Allah's forgiveness.

****

(١٥) عَنْ أَبِي هُرَيرَةَ رَضِيَ اللهُ عَنْهُ أَنَّ رَسُولَ اللهِ ﷺ قَالَ:

«قَالَ اللَّهُ: إِذَا أَحَبَّ عَبْدِي لِقَائِي أَحْبَبْتُ لِقَاءَهُ، وَإِذَا كَرِهَ لِقَائِي

كَرِهْتُ لِقَاءَهُ». «حديث صحيح» [رواه البخاري والنسائي]

He who loves to meet Allâh (by way of death like martyrs) Allâh too loves to meet him

15) Narrated Abû Huraira رضى الله عنه: Allâh's Messenger صلى الله عليه وسلم said that Allâh the Exalted observed: If My slave loves meeting Me, I too love meeting him. If he dislikes to meet Me, I too hate to meet him.

(This *Hadîth* is sound and reported by Bukhâri and Nasa'i).

This *Hadith* shows that a Muslim when he thinks of death he hopes to enter Paradise. So he likes death more or less. But disbelievers fear death because they do not have belief nor hope for Paradise. The believer who likes Paradise also likes death to meet Allah عز وجل . As a result, Allah عز وجل likes meeting him, too.

****

(١٦) عَنْ صَفْوَانِ بْنِ محرزِ المَازِنِي قَالَ: بَينَمَا أَنَا أَمْشِي مَعَ ابْنِ عُمَرَ رَضِيَ اللهُ عَنْهُمَا آخِذٌ بِيَدِهِ إِذْ عَرَضَ لَهُ رَجُلٌ فَقَالَ: كَيفَ سَمِعْتَ رَسُولَ اللهِ ﷺ فِي النَّجْوَى؟ فَقَالَ: سَمِعْتُ رَسُولَ اللهِ ﷺ يَقُولُ: «إِنَّ اللَّهَ يُدْنِي المُؤْمِنَ فَيَضَعُ عَلَيْهِ كَنَفَهُ وَيَسْتُرُهُ فَيَقُولُ أَتَعْرِفُ ذَنْبَ كَذَا أَتَعْرِفُ ذَنْبَ كَذَا فَيَقُولُ: نَعَمْ أَيْ رَبِّ حَتَّى إِذَا قَرَّرَهُ بِذُنُوبِهِ وَرَأَى فِي نَفْسِهِ أَنَّهُ هَلَكَ قَالَ سَتَرْتُهَا عَلَيْكَ فِي الدُّنْيَا وَأَنَا أَغْفِرُهَا لَكَ اليَوْمَ فَيُعْطَى كِتَابَ حَسَنَاتِهِ وَأَمَّا الكَافِرُ وَالْمُنَافِقُونَ فَيَقُولُ الأَشْهَادُ هَؤُلَاءِ الَّذِينَ كَذَبُوا عَلَى رَبِّهِمْ أَلَا لَعْنَةُ اللَّهِ عَلَى الظَّالِمِينَ».

«حديث صحيح» [رواه البخاري ومسلم وابن ماجه]

Allâh screens the believer in the world as well as in the Hereafter

16) Narrated Safwan bin Muhriz Al-Mazini: While I was on my way along with Ibn 'Umar رضى الله عنهما taking (holding up) his hand in mine. Suddenly a man appeared to him and said: What did you hear Allâh's Messenger صلى الله عليه وسلم

saying about confidential talk (secret conversation)? He said: I heard Allâh's Messenger صلى الله عليه وسلم saying: (On the Day of Resurrection) Allâh will draw near to a believer and put His forgiveness over him and screen him (his sins) then Allâh will say: Do you know such and such sin? Do you know such and such? He will say: Yes, my Lord! This conversation will continue) until Allâh will make him confess his sins, and thinks that he is ruined. Then Allâh will say: I concealed them (your sins in the world) and I do forgive you today. Then he will be given the record book containing his good deeds. As regards, the infidels and hypocrites, the witnesses will say: These are the people who have disbelieved their Lord. Behold! Allâh's Curse is upon transgressors.

(This *Hadîth* is sound and reported by Bukhâri, Muslim and Ibn Mâjah)

Allah's عز وجل mercy can be seen in this world. An evidence of this is that he covers the sinners though He is All-Mighty and All-Knowing. A further evidence is that he also forgives the same sins in the Hereafter. He عز وجل may also uncover you as a penalty in this world. So one should always care that Allâh is watching him.

****

(١٧) عَنْ أَبِي هُرَيرَةَ رَضِيَ اللهُ عَنْهُ عَنِ النَّبِيِّ ﷺ قَالَ: «قَالَ اللَّهُ عَزَّ وَجَلَّ: إِنَّ المُؤْمِنَ عِنْدِي بِمَنْزِلَةِ كُلِّ خَيْرٍ يَحْمَدُنِي وَأَنَا أَنْزِعُ نَفْسَهُ مِنْ بَيْنِ جَنْبَيْهِ». «حديث حسن» [رواه مسند أحمد]

Superiority of the believer

17) Narrated Abû Huraira رضى الله عنه The Prophet صلى الله عليه وسلم said: Allâh عز وجل said: Indeed a believer is in every good place with Me. He praises Me even when I take out his soul from between his sides.

(This *Hadîth* is sound and reported in *Musnad Ahmad*).

This *Hadith* highlights that Allah عز وجل appreciates the suffering of the believer when he dies and appreciates that much more for the one who though suffering the death, caused by Allah عز وجل , still attributes all praise to Allah عز وجل .

****

(١٨) عَنْ أَنَسِ بْنِ مَالِكٍ رَضِيَ اللهُ عَنْهُ قَالَ : قَالَ رَسُولُ اللهِ ﷺ : «قَالَ اللهُ عَزَّ وَجَلَّ : إِنَّ أُمَّتَكَ لاَ يَزَالُونَ يَقُولُونَ مَا كَذَا؟ مَا كَذَا؟ حَتَّى يَقُولُوا : هَذَا اللهُ خَلَقَ الخَلْقَ فَمَنْ خَلَقَ اللهُ» .

«حديث صحيح» [رواه مسلم]

Devil's promptings

18) Narrated Anas bin Mâlik رضي الله عنه: Allâh's Messenger said: Allâh عزوجل said: Your followers will still remain saying: What is that? What is that? until they say: It is Allâh who has created the creation then who created Allâh ?

(This *Hadîth* is sound and reported by Muslim).

The devil plays a role in making people disbelievers by such questions about Allah عز وجل . Before we deal with such questions of the devil which nobody can answer, let us ask ourselves a question: Do we know every thing about the creatures so that we ask about the Creator. The creature can never know how to answer a question of this type about Allah عز وجل . Allah created us but Allah's existence is evident for all of us; His existence was all by Himself. The "How" of this matter is beyond the perception of the human mind so it is a pointless question to ask, but the devil aims at making people go astray. If you have any such whisperings of the devil, you can ask Allah عز وجل to protect you and say: "I believe in Allah and His Messenger."

****

(١٩) عَنْ أَبِي سَعِيْدٍ الخُدْرِيِّ وَأَبِي هُرَيرَةَ رَضِيَ اللهُ عَنْهُمَا

قَالَ : قَالَ رَسُولُ اللهِ ﷺ : يَقُولُ اللهُ عَزَّوَجَلَّ «الْعِزُّ إِزَارِي وَالْكِبْرِيَاءُ رِدَائِي فَمَنْ يُنَازِعُنِي عَذَّبْتُهُ» . « حديث صحيح »

[رواه مسلم وابن ماجه وأبو داؤود]

Prohibition of Pride and Vanity

19) Narrated Abû Sa'îd Al-Khudri and Abû Huraira: Allâh's Messenger صلى الله عليه وسلم said: Glory is Allah's loin cloth and pride is His cloak. Allâh says: He who contends with Me in regard to them, I will torment him.

Pride and Glory are qualities of Allah عز وجل so, a Muslim should always be humble and should not attach these qualities to himself whatsoever.

(This *Hadith* is sound and reported by Muslim, Ibn Mâjah and Abu Dâ'ud).

****

(٢٠) عَنْ أَبِي هُرَيرَةَ رَضِيَ اللهُ عَنْهُ قَالَ : قَالَ رَسُولُ اللهِ ﷺ : «قَالَ اللهُ عَزَّ وَجَلَّ : يُؤْذِيْنِي ابْنُ آدَمَ يَسُبُّ الدَّهْرَ وَأَنَا الدَّهْرُ، بِيَدِي الأَمْرُ أُقَلِّبُ اللَّيْلَ وَالنَّهَارَ» . «حديث صحيح»

[رواه البخاري ومسلم وأبو داؤود والنسائي]

Prohibition of Abusing Time

20) Narrated Abû Huraira رضى الله عنه: Allâh's Messenger صلى الله عليه وسلم said: Allâh عزوجل said: The son of Adam displeases Me by abusing the time whereas I am Myself the time. In My Hand lay all the things and I am the one who causes the revolution of the day and night.

(This *Hadîth* is sound and reported by Bukhâri,

Muslim, Abû Dâ'ud and Nasa'i).

Once Allah عز وجل causes the day and night and controls time, abusing time is a bad deed that should not happen. Precisely, abusing time is not permissible in Islam.

****

(٢١) عَنْ أَبِي هُرَيرَةَ رَضِيَ اللهُ عَنْهُ عَنِ النَّبِيِّ ﷺ قَالَ : «قَالَ اللهُ تَعَالَى : كَذَّبَنِي ابْنُ آدَمَ وَلَمْ يَكُنْ لَهُ ذٰلِكَ وَشَتَمَنِي وَلَمْ يَكُنْ لَهُ ذٰلِكَ فَأَمَّا تَكْذِيبُه إِيَّايَ فَقَوْلُهُ لَنْ يُعِيدَنِي كَمَا بَدَأَنِي وَلَيْسَ أَوَّلُ الْخَلْقِ بِأَهْوَنَ عَلَيَّ مِنْ إِعَادَتِهِ، وَأَمَّا شَتْمُهُ إِيَّايَ فَقَوْلُه اتَّخَذَ اللهُ وَلَدًا وَأَنَا الأَحَدُ الصَّمَدُ لَمْ أَلِدْ وَلَمْ أُوْلَدْ وَلَمْ يَكُنْ لِي كُفُوًا أَحَدٌ» . «حديث صحيح» [رواه البخاري ومسلم]

Son of Adam tells a lie against his Lord and abuses him

21) Narrated Abû Huraira رضي الله عنه: The Prophet صلى الله عليه وسلم said: Allâh تعالى said: The son of Adam disbelieves in Me though he ought not and he abuses Me though he has no right for that. As for his disbelieving in Me, it is his statement that He will not be resurrected as was created, though his recreation is easier to Me than the first creation. As for his abusing Me, it is his say that Allâh has a son, but I am the One, the Everlasting. Neither I have begotten nor have been begotten nor do I have any match.

(This *Hadîth* is sound and reported by Bukhâri and Nasa'i).

Making associates to Allah عز وجل is in a way, calling Allah عز وجل by bad names. Allah عز وجل is the One and the only God.

(٢٢) عَنْ عَبْدِ الرَّحْمٰنِ بْنِ قَتَادَةَ السَّلْمِيِّ أَنَّهُ قَالَ : سَمِعْتُ رَسُولَ اللهِ ﷺ يَقُولُ : «إِنَّ اللهَ عَزَّ وَجَلَّ خَلَقَ آدَمَ ثُمَّ أَخَذَ الخَلْقَ مِنْ ظَهْرِهِ وَقَالَ : هَؤُلاَءِ فِي الجَنَّةِ وَلاَ أُبَالِي ، وَهَؤُلاَءِ فِي النَّارِ وَلاَ أُبَالِي ، فَقَالَ قَائِلٌ : يَارَسُوْلَ اللهِ فَعَلَى مَاذَا نَعْمَلُ قَالَ : عَلَى مَوَاقِعِ الْقَدَرِ» . «حديث حسن» [رواه مسند أحمد]

Everybody will do according to his destiny

22) Abdur-Rahman bin Qatada As-Salami said: I heard the Prophet صلى الله عليه و سلم saying: Allâh created Adam, took his progeny from his back and said: These will go to Hell and these will go to Paradise. Somebody said, the narrator added: O Messenger of Allâh, what shall we do then? The Prophet said: You will do according to your destiny.

(This *Hadîth* is good and narrated by Ahmad).

Allâh is the All-Knower, so He took everybody to Hell or Paradise as per His Knowledge of what will happen in the future, in other words, one's destiny was known to Allâh but to him it is absolutely unknown.

****

(٢٣) عَنْ أَبِي هُرَيرَةَ قَالَ : قَالَ رَسُولُ اللهِ ﷺ : «أَلَمْ تَرَوْا إِلَى مَا قَالَ رَبُّكُمْ؟ قَالَ : مَا أَنْعَمْتُ عَلَى عِبَادِي مِنْ نِعْمَةٍ إِلاَّ أَصْبَحَ فَرِيْقٌ مِنْهُمْ بِهَا كَافِرِيْنَ يَقُوْلُوْنَ : اَلْكَوَاكِبُ وَبِالْكَوَاكِبِ» .

«حديث صحيح» [رواه مسلم والنسائي]

Superiority of disbelief in Stars

23) Abû Huraira رضى الله عنه narrated, the Prophet صلى الله عليه و سلم

said: Allâh said: Whenever I bestow something on my slaves some of them turn as blasphemers and say: The planets and by the planets.

(This *Hadîth* is sound and narrated by Muslim and Nasa'i).

This *Hadîth* highlights the wrong attribution the disbelievers make to the endowments of Allâh e.g. they think that such things and gifts are caused by the stars and planets. What a wrong belief!

****

(٢٤) عَنْ أَبِي هُرَيرَةَ رَضِيَ اللهُ قَالَ: مَرَّ رَسُولُ اللهِ ﷺ عَلَى رَهْطٍ مِنْ أَصْحَابِهِ وَهُمْ يَضْحَكُونَ فقَالَ: «لَوْ تَعْلَمُوْنَ مَا أَعْلَمُ لَضَحِكْتُمْ قَلِيْلاً وَلَبَكَيْتُمْ كَثِيْرًا، فَأَتَاهُ جِبْرِيْلُ فقَالَ: إِنَّ اللهَ يَقُوْلُ لَكَ: لِمَ تُقَنِّطُ عِبَادِى؟ قَالَ فَرَجَعَ إِلَيْهِمْ فقَالَ: سَدِّدُوْا وَأَبْشِرُوْا». «إسناده صحيح» [رواه ابن حبان في الزوائد]

Discouragement of Desparation

24) Abû Huraira رضى الله عنه said: Allâh's Messenger صلى الله عليه وسلم passed while some of his Companions were laughing. He said to them: If you know what I know you should laugh very little and weep a lot. Then Jibrael came to him and said: Allâh says to you: Do not make my slaves feel desparate (from my mercy). Then the Prophet صلى الله عليه وسلم came back and said to us: Be hopeful, be happy.

(The chain of narrators is sound and narrated by Ibn Hiban.)

There is always hope as far as we believe that the mercy of Allâh supercedes His anger.

****

(٢٥) عَنْ أَبِي هُرَيرَةَ رَضِيَ اللهُ عَنْهُ أَنَّ رَسُولَ اللهِ ﷺ قَالَ:

«لَمَّا خَلَقَ اللهُ الجَنَّةَ قَالَ لِجِبْرِيلَ: اذْهَبْ فَانْظُرْ إِلَيْهَا فَذَهَبَ فَنَظَرَ إِلَيْهَا ثُمَّ جَاءَ فَقَالَ: أَيْ رَبِّ وَعِزَّتِكَ لاَ يَسْمَعُ بِهَا أَحَدٌ إِلاَّ دَخَلَهَا. ثُمَّ حَفَّهَا بِالْمَكَارِهِ ثُمَّ قَالَ: يَا جِبْرِيلُ اذْهَبْ فَانْظُرْ إِلَيْهَا فَذَهَبَ فَنَظَرَ إِلَيْهَا ثُمَّ جَاءَ فَقَالَ: أَيْ رَبِّ وَعِزَّتِكَ لَقَدْ خَشِيتُ أَنْ لاَ يَدْخُلَهَا أَحَدٌ. قَالَ: فَلَمَّا خَلَقَ النَّارَ قَالَ: يَاجِبْرِيلُ اذْهَبْ فَانْظُرْ إِلَيْهَا فَذَهَبَ فَنَظَرَ إِلَيْهَا ثُمَّ جَاءَ فَقَالَ: أَيْ رَبِّ وَعِزَّتِكَ لاَ يَسْمَعُ بِهَا أَحَدٌ فَيَدْخُلُهَا فَحَفَّهَا بِالشَّهَوَاتِ ثُمَّ قَالَ: يَاجِبْرِيلُ اذْهَبْ فَانْظُرْ إِلَيْهَا فَذَهَبَ إِلَيْهَا ثُمَّ جَاءَ فَقَالَ: أَيْ رَبِّ وَعِزَّتِكَ لَقَدْ خَشِيتُ أَنْ لاَ يَبْقَى أَحَدٌ إِلاَّ دَخَلَهَا». «حديث حسن»

[رواه أبو داوود والترمذي والنسائي وأحمد والحاكم]

Paradise is surrounded with hardships whereas Hell is encompassed with lusts

25) Narrated Abû Huraira رضى الله عنه that Allâh's Messenger صلى الله عليه وسلم said: When Allâh created Paradise, He ordered Jibrael: Go and see it. So he went and saw it. Then he returned and said: O Lord, By Your glory! who hears of it would love entering it. Then He encompassed it with unpleasant things (hardships of worship) and said: O Jibrael! Go (again) and see it. So he went away to look at it. Then he came back and said: O Lord, By Your glory! I fear that no one will enter it. The Prophet صلى الله عليه وسلم said: When Allâh created Hell, He said: O Jibrael, go and see it.

So he went and saw it. Then he turned up and said: O Lord, By Your glory! No one who hears of it will enter it. So he encompassed it with lusts (worldy desires) and said: O Jibrael! Go back and see it. He went again to see it and came back saying: O Lord, By Your glory! I fear that no one will escape from entering it

(This *Hadîth* is fair and reported by Abû Dâ'ud, Tirmidhi, Nasa'i, Ahmad in *Musnad* and Al-Hâkim in *Mustadrak*)

Allah has promised to give Paradise in reward to those who do good deeds for His sake. But man is misguided by the Satan and worldly lusts which cause him to do bad deeds that lead to Hell. He who undergoes hardships in the cause of Allah; these hardships will lead him to the enternal abode of pleasures.

****

(٢٦) عَنْ أَبِي هُرَيْرَةَ رَضِيَ اللهُ عَنْهُ عَنْ رَسُولِ اللهِ ﷺ قَالَ : «قَالَ اللهُ تَبَارَكَ وَتَعَالَى : أَعْدَدْتُ لِعِبَادِي الصَّالِحِيْنَ مَا لاَ عَيْنٌ رَأَتْ وَلاَ أُذُنٌ سَمِعَتْ وَلاَ خَطَرَ عَلَى قَلْبِ بَشَرٍ» .

«حديث صحيح» [رواه البخاري ومسلم والترمذي وابن ماجه]

Some of what Allâh has prepared for His righteous slaves

26) Narrated Abû Huraira رضى الله عنه the Prophet صلى الله عليه وسلم said: Allâh عز وجل said: I had prepared for My righteous slaves what no eye has seen nor any ear has heard nor any human mind has realised (nor it has occurred to any human heart).

(This *Hadîth* is sound and reported by Bukhâri, Muslim,Tirmidhi and Ibn Mâjah).

Later on Abû Huraira said: Recite if you wish: No soul knows about the joy of eyes (pleasure) which has been hidden for them.

What Allah سبحانه و تعالى has prepared for the believers in *Jannah* (Paradise) is beyond any description, imagination or perception. What we read of that in the Noble Qur'ân is only what the human brain can perceive. But *Jannah* is beyond all that.

****

(٢٧) عَنْ أَبِي سَعِيدٍ الْخُدْرِيِّ رَضِيَ اللهُ عَنْهُ قَالَ: قَالَ النَّبِيُّ ﷺ: «إِنَّ اللهَ يَقُوْلُ لأَهْلِ الْجَنَّةِ: يَا أَهْلَ الْجَنَّةِ فَيَقُولُونَ لَبَّيْكَ رَبَّنَا وَسَعْدَيْكَ وَالْخَيْرُ فِي يَدَيْكَ فَيَقُوْلُ: هَلْ رَضِيْتُمْ؟ فَيَقُوْلُوْنَ وَمَالَنَا لاَ نَرْضَى يَارَبِّ وَقَدْ أَعْطَيْتَنَا مَا لَمْ تُعْطِ أَحَدًا مِنْ خَلْقِكَ فَيَقُوْلُ: أَلاَ أُعْطِيْكُمْ أَفْضَلَ مِنْ ذٰلِكَ؟ فَيَقُوْلُونَ: يَارَبِّ وَأَيُّ شَيْءٍ أَفْضَلُ مِنْ ذٰلِكَ؟ فَيَقُوْلُ: أُحِلُّ عَلَيْكُمْ رِضْوَانِي فَلاَ أَسْخَطُ عَلَيْكُمْ بَعْدَهُ أَبَدًا». «حديث صحيح»

[رواه البخاري ومسلم]

Allâh's pleasure for the inhabitants of Paradise

27) Narrated Abû Sa'îd Al-Khudri رضى الله عنه: Prophet Muhammad صلى الله عليه وسلم said: Verily, Allâh will address the inhabitants of Paradise: O inhabitants of Paradise! They will say: We do respond and are at Your pleasure; and goodness rests in Your Hand. He will ask them: Are you satisfied? They will say: Why should we not be satisfied, O Lord! while You have given us what You have not given to anyone of Your creation? Then He will say: Would you not like Me to grant you something better than that? They will say: O Lord! What is better than that? He will say: I will never be angry with you afterwards.

(This *Hadîth* is sound and reported by Bukhâri and Muslim).

****

(٢٨) عَنْ أَبِي هُرَيرَةَ رَضِيَ اللهُ عَنْهُ أَنَّ النَّبِيَّ ﷺ كَانَ يَوْمًا يُحَدِّثُ وَعِنْدَهُ رَجُلٌ مِنْ أَهْلِ الْبَادِيَةِ «أَنَّ رَجُلاً مِنْ أَهْلِ الْجَنَّةِ اسْتَأْذَنَ رَبَّهُ فِي الزَّرْعِ فَقَالَ: أَوَ لَسْتَ فِيْمَا شِئْتَ؟ قَالَ: بَلَى وَلكِنِّي أُحِبُّ أَنْ أَزْرَعَ فَأَسْرَعَ وَبَذَرَ فَتَبَادَرَ الطَّرْفَ نَبَاتُهُ وَاسْتِوَاؤُهُ وَاسْتِحْصَاؤُهُ وَتَكْوِيزُهُ أَمْثَالَ الْجِبَالِ فَيَقُوْلُ اللهُ تَعَالَى: وَذٰلِكَ يَاابْنَ آدَمَ فَإِنَّهُ لاَ يُشْبِعُكَ شَيْءٌ». فَقَالَ الأَعْرَابِيُّ: يَارَسُوْلَ اللهِ لاَنَجِدُ هَذَا إِلاَّ قُرَشِيًا أَوْ أَنْصَارِيًّا فَإِنَّهُمْ أَصْحَابُ زَرْعٍ فَأَمَّا نَحْنُ فَلَسْنَا بِأَصْحَابِ زَرْعٍ فَضَحِكَ رَسُوْلُ اللهِ ﷺ.

«حديث صحيح» [رواه البخاري]

Inhabitants of Paradise will be given pursuit

28) Narrated Abû Huraira رضى الله عنه that the Prophet صلى الله عليه وسلم was narrating a *Hadîth* while a Bedouin was in his company: One of the inhabitants of Paradise will seek permission from his Lord for cultivation. Allâh will ask him: What do you wish? He will reply in affirmative and say: But I like to cultivate (the land). (When the man is permitted) he will soon sow the seeds. The plants will grow up, get ripe and be ready for harvesting. Then the yield will develop into conglobation like huge mountains then Allâh عز وجل will say: O son of Adam! Nothing can satisfy you. At this, the Bedouin remarked: O Allâh's Messenger! This man must be either from Quraish (i.e. an

emigrant) or an Ansari (resident of Al-Madina) because they are cultivators whereas we are not (on hearing it) Allâh's Messenger صلى الله عليه وسلم laughed.

(This *Hadîth* is sound and reported by Bukhâri.)

****

(٢٩) عَنْ عَبْدِ اللهِ بْنِ مَسْعُودٍ رَضِيَ اللهُ عَنْهُ قَالَ: قَالَ رَسُولُ اللهِ ﷺ: «آخِرُ مَنْ يَدْخُلُ الْجَنَّةَ رَجُلٌ فَهُوَ يَمْشِي مَرَّةً وَيَكْبُوْ مَرَّةً وتَسْعَفُهُ النَّارُ مَرَّةً فَإِذَا مَا جَاوَزَهَا الْتَفَتَ إِلَيْهَا فَقَالَ: تَبَارَكَ الَّذِي نَجَّانِي مِنْك لَقَدْ أَعْطَانِى اللهُ شَيْئًا مَا أَعْطَاهُ أَحَدًا مِنَ الأَوَّلِيْنَ وَالآخِرِيْنَ فَتُرْفَعُ لَهُ شَجَرَةٌ فَيَقُوْلُ أَيْ رَبِّ أَدْنِنِي مِنْ هَذِهِ الشَّجَرَةِ فَلأَسْتَظِلَّ بِظِلِّهَا وَأَشْرَبُ مِنْ مَائِهَا فَيَقُوْلُ اللهُ عَزَّ وَجَلَّ: يَاابْنَ آدَمَ لَعَلِّى إِنْ أَعْطَيْتُكَها سَأَلْتَنِي غَيْرَهَا فَيَقُوْلُ: لاَ يَارَبِّ وَيُعَاهِدُهُ أَنْ لاَ يَسْأَلَهُ غَيْرَهَا وَرَبُّهُ يعذرُهُ لأَنَّهُ يَرَى مَا لاَ صَبْرَ عَلَيْهِ فَيُدْنِيْهِ مِنْهَا فَيَسْتَظِلُّ بِظِلِّهَا وَيَشْرَبُ مِنْ مَائِهَا ثُمَّ تُرْفَعُ لَهُ شَجَرَةٌ هِيَ أَحْسَنُ مِنَ الأُوْلَى فَيَقُوْلُ: أَيْ رَبِّ أَدْنِنِي مِنْ هَذِهِ لأَشْرَبَ مِنْ مَائِهَا وَأَسْتَظِلَّ بِظِلِّهَا لاَ أَسْأَلُكَ غَيْرَهَا فَيَقُوْلُ: يَاابْنَ آدَمَ أَلَمْ تُعَاهِدْنِيْ أَنْ لاَ تَسْأَلَنِيْ غَيْرَهَا؟ فَيَقُوْلُ: لَعَلِّي إِنْ أَدْنَيْتُكَ مِنْهَا تَسْأَلْنِي غَيْرَهَا فَيُعَاهِدُهُ أَنْ لاَ يَسْأَلَهُ غَيْرَهَا وَرَبُّهُ يعذرُهُ لأَنَّهُ يَرَى مَا لاَ صَبْرَ عَلَيْهِ فَيُدْنِيْهِ مِنْهَا فَيَسْتَظِلُّ بِظِلِّهَا وَيَشْرَبُ مِنْ مَائِهَا ثُمَّ تُرْفَعُ لَهُ

شَجَرَةٌ عَنْدَ بَابِ الْجَنَّةِ هِيَ أَحْسَنُ مِنَ الأُوْلَيَيْنِ فَيَقُوْلُ: أَيْ رَبِّ؟ أَدْنِنِي مِنْ هَذِهِ لأَسْتَظِلَّ بِظِلِّهَا وَأَشْرَبَ مِنْ مَائِهَا لاَ أَسْأَلُكَ غَيْرَهَا وَرَبُّهُ يعذرُهُ لأَنَّهُ يَرَى مَا صَبْرَ لَهُ عَلَيْهَا فَيُدْنِيْهِ مِنْهَا فَإِذَا أَدْنَاهُ مِنْهَا فَيَسْمَعُ أَصْوَاتَ أَهْلِ الجَنَّةِ فَيَقُوْلُ: أَيْ رَبِّ أَدْخِلْنِيْهَا فَيَقُوْلُ: يَاابْنَ آدَمَ مَا يَصْرِيْنِي مِنْكَ؟ أَيُرْضِيْكَ أَنْ أُعْطِيَكَ الدُّنْيَا وَمِثْلَهَا مَعَهَا قَالَ: يَارَبِّ أَتَسْتَهْزِيءُ مِنِّي وَأَنْتَ رَبُّ الْعَالَمِيْنَ».

فَضَحِكَ ابْنُ مَسْعُوْدٍ فَقَالَ أَلاَ تَسْأَلُوْنِي مِمَّ أَضْحَكُ؟ فَقَالُوْا: مِمَّ تَضْحَكُ قَالَ هَكَذَا ضَحِكَ رَسُوْلُ اللهِ ﷺ فَقَالُوْا: مِمَّا تَضْحَكُ يَارَسُوْلَ اللهِ قَالَ: «مِنْ ضَحِكِ رَبِّ الْعَالَمِيْنَ حِيْنَ قَالَ أَتَسْتَهْزِيءُ مِنِّي وَأَنْتَ رَبُّ الْعَالَمِيْنَ فَيَقُوْلُ: إِنِّي لاَ أَسْتَهْزِيءُ مِنْكَ وَلَكِنِّي عَلَى مَا أَشَاءُ قَادِرٌ».

«حديث صحيح» [رواه مسلم]

The last to enter Paradise

29) Narrated ‘Abdullâh bin Mas‘ûd رضى الله عنه: Allâh’s Messenger صلى الله عليه وسلم said: The last entrant to Paradise would be a man who walks once and stumbles once and be burnt by the fire once. When he gets beyond it, he will turn to it and say: Blessed is He who has saved me from you and has given me what He gave nobody in the earlier or later times. Then a tree would be raised up for him. So he will

say: O my Lord! bring me closer to this tree so that I may take shelter in its shade and drink from its water. Allâh عز وجل would say: O son of Adam! If I grant you this, you will demand Me something else. He will say: No, my Lord. He promised that he would ask for nothing else. His Lord would excuse him because He sees that the man would not have patience over it. So He will make him near it. Then he will take shelter in its shade and drink its water. Afterwards, a tree more beautiful than the first would be raised up before him. So he will say: O my Lord! Bring me near this tree. So that I may drink its water and take shelter in its shade. I shall not ask you for anything other than that. Allâh will say: O son of Adam! Did you not promise Me that you would not ask Me for anything else. He will reply: Probably I shall ask for nothing if you bring me near it. And he promised Him that he would not ask Him for anything else. His Lord would excuse him because He knows that he would not keep his word. Anyhow, He would bring him near to the tree. The man will take shelter in its shade and drink its water. Then a tree more beautiful than the first two would be raised up at the gate of Paradise. He will say: O Lord! Please make me near to this tree so that I may enjoy its shade and drink its water. I shall not ask You anything else. His Lord would excuse him as the temptation of which he could not resist. So He will make him near this tree. When He would bring him near it, he would hear the voices of the inhabitants of Paradise. He would say: O my Lord! Admit me to it. Allâh would say: O son of Adam! What will bring an end to your demands to Me? Will it please you if I give you the (whole) world and a similar one along with it? The man will say: Are you mocking at me, though you are the Lord of the worlds?

Narrating this *Hadîth* Ibn Mas'ûd laughed and asked (the hearers): Why don't you ask me what I am laughing at. They said: Why do you laugh? He said: In the same way Allâh's

Messenger صلى الله عليه وسلم also laughed (when he said this *Hadith*, and (the Companions) asked: Why do you laugh, O Messenger of Allâh? He replied: On account of the laughter of the Lord of the worlds when the desirous of Paradise said: Are you mocking at me though you are the Lord of the worlds? At this, Allah will remark: I am not mocking at you, but I am All-Capable to do whatever I wish.

(This *Hadîth* is sound and reported by Muslim).

This *Hadith* highlights the fact that the last entrant to Paradise will undergo various phases. It also shows the aspect of human nature that man is not contended with one thing but always desires better than that is available to him.

****

(٣٠) عَنْ أَبِي ذَرٍّ رَضِيَ اللهُ عَنْهُ قَالَ: قَالَ رَسُولُ اللهِ ﷺ: «إِنِّي لأَعْرِفُ آخِرَ أَهْلِ النَّارِ خُرُوْجًا مِنَ النَّارِ وَآخِرَ أَهْلِ الْجَنَّةِ دُخُوْلاً الجَنَّةَ يُؤْتَى بِرَجُلٍ فَيَقُوْلُ: سَلُوْا عَنْ صِغَارِ ذُنُوْبِهِ وَاخْبَئُوْا كِبَارَهَا فَيُقَالُ لَهُ عَمِلْتَ كَذَا وَكَذَا فِي يَوْمِ كَذَا وَكَذَا عَمِلْتَ كَذَا وَكَذَا فِي يَوْمِ كَذَا وَكَذَا قَالَ فَيُقَالُ لَهُ: فَإِنَّ لَكَ مَكَانُ كُلِّ سَيِّئَةٍ حَسَنَة قَالَ: فَيَقُوْلُ: يَارَبِّ لَقَدْ عَمِلْتُ أَشْيَاءَ مَا أَرَاهَا هَاهُنَا» قَالَ فَلَقَدْ رَأَيْتُ رَسُوْلَ اللهِ ﷺ ضَحِكَ حَتَّى بَدَتْ نَوَاجِذُهُ. «حديث صحيح» [رواه الترمذي]

30) Narrated Abû Dhar رضى الله عنه: Allâh's Messenger صلى الله عليه وسلم said: I know the last of the dwellers of Hell to come out and the last of the people of Paradise to enter. He is a man who would be brought before Allah on the Day of Resurrection. Then Allâh will command the angels: Ask

him about the minor sins and hide the major ones. Then it will be said to him: On such and such day you did that and that sin; and on such and such day you committed that and that bad deed. The Prophet صلى الله عليه وسلم added: It will be said to him: In place of every evil deed, you will be granted one good deed. The Prophet صلى الله عليه وسلم continued. The sinner would say: My Lord! I have done things which I do not find here. The narrator said: Indeed I saw the Messenger of Allâh صلى الله عليه وسلم laugh until his premolar teeth were visible. (because the sinner was frogiven.)

(This *Hadîth* is sound and reported by Tirmidhi).

This is how Allah would cover a sinner with His Mercy. Even his minor sins would be so great that he will feel so ashamed of them that he will not be able to ask Allah Paradise.

****

(٣١) عَنْ مَسْرُوقٍ قَالَ: سَأَلْنَا عَبْدُ اللهِ بْنِ مَسْعُودٍ عَنْ هٰذِهِ الآيَةِ ﴿وَلاَ تَحْسَبَنَّ الَّذِيْنَ قُتِلُوْا فِي سَبِيْلِ اللهِ أَمْوَاتًا، بَلْ أَحْيَاءٌ عِنْدَ رَبِّهِمْ يُرْزَقُوْنَ﴾ قَالَ أَمَّا إِنَّا قَدْ سَأَلْنَا عَنْ ذٰلِكَ فَقَالَ: «أَرْوَاحُهُمْ فِي جَوْفِ طَيْرٍ خُضْرٍ لَهَا قَنَادِيْلُ مُعَلَّقَةٌ بِالْعَرْشِ تَسْرَحُ مِنَ الْجَنَّةِ حَيْثُ شَاءَتْ ثُمَّ تَأْوِي إِلَى تِلْكَ الْقَنَادِيْلِ فَاطَّلَعَ إِلَيْهِم رَبُّهُمْ اِطِّلاَعَةً فَقَالَ: هَلْ تَشْتَهُوْنَ شَيْئًا؟ قَالُوْا: أَيُّ شَيْءٍ نَشْتَهِيْ؟ وَنَحْنُ نَسْرَحُ مِنَ الْجَنَّةِ حَيْثُ شِئْنَا فَفُعِلَ ذٰلِكَ بِهِمْ ثَلاَثَ مَرَّاتٍ فَلَمَّا رَأَوْا أَنَّهُمْ لَنْ يُتْرَكُوْا مِنْ أَنْ يُسْأَلُوْا قَالُوْا يَا رَبِّ نُرِيْدُ أَنْ تُرَدَّ أَرْوَاحُنَا فِي أَجْسَادِنَا حَتَّى نُقْتَلَ فِي سَبِيْلِكَ مَرَّةً أُخْرَى، فَلَمَّا رَأَى أَنْ لَيْسَ لَهُمْ حَاجَةٌ تُرِكُوْا».

«حديث صحيح» [رواه مسلم]

Superiority of martyrs

31) Narrated Masrûq: We asked 'Abdullâh bin Mas'ûd (رضى الله عنه) about this verse:

> "Think not of those who have been killed in the way of Allâh as dead; rather they are alive with their Lord being provided with sustenance." (3:169)

He (Abdullâh bin Mas'ûd رضى الله عنه) said: We asked the Prophet صلى الله عليه وسلم the meaning of this verse. So he explained it like this:

Their souls are inside some green birds beside lanterns suspended from the Divine Throne roaming freely in Paradise wherever they like. Then they take shelter at those lanterns. Once their Lord looked at them and said: Do you want anything else? They said: What more shall we want? We roam freely in Paradise as we like. Allâh asked them the same question three times. When they felt that they would not be spared from being asked, they said: O Lord! We like You to put back our souls into our bodies so that we may be killed in Your way once again. As Allâh saw that they had no wish, they would be let for joy in heaven.

(This *Hadîth* is sound and reported by Bukhâri).

A *Shaheed* is a martyr who fought for the sake of Allah عز وجل and was killed. His grade in Paradise is next to a *Siddiq* i.e. one who was a forerunner and first to believe in His Prophet. (e.g. Abu Bakr رضي الله عنه). The grades are: Prophets then the *Siddiqun* then the martyrs, then the righteous ones. This *Hadith* alongwith No. 41,42 and 43 highlight the graces Allah عز وجل shall bestow on the martyrs in the Hereafter and even in their graves before resurrection.

****

(٣٢) عَنْ أَنَسٍ رَضِيَ اللهُ عَنْهُ قَالَ: قَالَ رَسُولُ اللهِ ﷺ:

«يُؤْتَى بِالرَّجُلِ مِنْ أَهْلِ الجَنَّةِ فَيَقُوْلُ اللهُ عَزَّ وَجَلَّ: يَاابْنَ آدَمَ

كَيْفَ وَجَدْتَ مَنْزِلَكَ؟ فَيَقُوْلُ: أَيْ رَبِّ خَيْرَ مَنْزِلٍ فَيَقُوْلُ: سَلْ وَتَمَنَّ فَيَقُوْلُ: أَسْأَلُكَ أَنْ تَرُدَّنِي إِلَى الدُّنْيَا فَأُقْتَلُ فِي سَبِيْلِكَ عَشَرَ مَرَّاتٍ لِمَا يَرَى مِنْ فَضْلِ الشَّهَادَةِ».

«حديث صحيح» [رواه النسائي]

32) Narrated Anas رضى الله عنه: Allâh's Messenger صلى الله عليه وسلم said: A man from among people of Paradise will be brought forward. Allâh عز وجل will ask him: O Son of Adam! How did you find your home? He will reply: O my Lord! It is the best home, then Allâh will say: Ask and wish anything you like. The man will say: I would ask You to send me back to the world in order to be killed in Your way ten times. (This is because of the superiority of the martyrdom and the high position which martyrs would be made to occupy in heaven).

(This *Hadîth* is sound and reported by Nasa'i).

****

(٣٣) عَنِ ابْنِ عُمَرَ رَضِيَ اللهُ عَنْهُمَا عَنِ النَّبِيِّ ﷺ فِيمَا يَحْكِي عَنْ رَبِّهِ تَبَارَكَ وَتَعَالَى قَالَ: «أَيُّمَا عَبْدٍ مِنْ عِبَادِي خَرَجَ مُجَاهِدًا فِي سَبِيْلِي ابْتِغَاءَ مَرْضَاتِي ضَمِنْتُ لَهُ أَنْ أُرْجِعَهُ بِمَا أَصَابَ مِنْ أَجْرٍ وَغَنِيْمَةٍ وَإِنْ قَبَضْتُهُ أَنْ أَغْفِرَ لَهُ وَأَرْحَمَهُ وَأُدْخِلَهُ الجَنَّةَ». «حديث صحيح لغيره» [رواه مسند أحمد]

33) Narrated Ibn 'Umar رضى الله عنهما Prophet صلى الله عليه وسلم quoted his Lord عز وجل as saying: Whoever of My slaves comes out to fight in My way seeking My pleasure, I guarantee him that I will compensate his suffering with reward and booty (during

his lifetime) and if he dies, I would forgive him, have mercy on him and let him enter Paradise.

(This *Hadîth* is fairly sound and reported in *Musnad Ahmad*).

A soldier who fights in the way of Allah will be best rewarded by Allah in this world as well as in the Hereafter.

****

(٣٤) عَنِ ابْنِ عَبَّاسٍ رَضِيَ اللهُ عَنْهُمَا قَالَ: قَالَ رَسُولُ اللهِ ﷺ: «لَمَّا أُصِيبَ إِخْوَانُكُمْ بِأُحُدٍ جَعَلَ اللهُ أَرْوَاحَهُمْ فِي جَوْفِ طَيْرٍ خُضْرٍ تَرِدُ أَنْهَارَ الْجَنَّةِ تَأْكُلُ مِنْ ثِمَارِهَا وَتَأْوِي إِلَى قَنَادِيلَ مِنْ ذَهَبٍ مُعَلَّقَةٍ فِي ظِلِّ الْعَرْشِ فَلَمَّا وَجَدُوا طِيبَ مَأْكَلِهِمْ وَمَشْرَبِهِمْ وَمَقِيلِهِمْ قَالُوا مَنْ يُبَلِّغُ إِخْوَانَنَا عَنَّا أَنَّا أَحْيَاءٌ فِي الْجَنَّةِ نُرْزَقُ لِئَلَّا يَزْهَدُوا فِي الْجِهَادِ وَلاَ يَنْكُلُوا عِنْدَ الْحَرْبِ؟ فَقَالَ اللهُ سُبْحَانَهُ: أَنَا أُبَلِّغُهُمْ عَنْكُمْ. قَالَ فَأَنْزَلَ اللهُ ﴿وَلاَ تَحْسَبَنَّ الَّذِينَ قُتِلُوا فِي سَبِيلِ اللهِ. . . .﴾

«حديث حسن» [رواه أبو داؤود]

Reason of revelation of Allâh's Statement on martyrs

34) Narrated Ibn 'Abbâs رضى الله عنهما: Allâh's Messenger صلى الله عليه وسلم said: When your brethren were killed as martyrs in the battle of Uhud, Allâh put their souls into some green birds which arrived at the rivers of Paradise, ate from its fruits and took shelter beside lanterns, made of gold, and suspended in the shade of the Divine Throne. When they enjoued eating, drinking and sleeping, they said: Who will

convey to our brethren on earth that: we are alive in Paradise where we are provided with sustenance, so that they would neither renounce fighting in the way of Allâh nor retreat at the time of war. Allâh the Glorified said: I shall inform them of you. The Prophet صلى الله عليه وسلم said: So Allâh revealed this verse:

> "Don't consider those killed in the way of Allâh as dead, rather they are alive with their Lord being provided with sustenance".(3:169)

(This *Hadîth* is good and reported in *Sunan Abi Dâ'ud*).

****

(٣٥) عَنْ عَيَاضِ بْنِ حِمَارٍ الْمُجَاشِعِي أَنَّ رَسُولَ اللهِ ﷺ قَالَ ذَاتَ يَوْمٍ فِي خُطْبَتِهِ: «أَلاَ إِنَّ رَبِّي أَمَرَنِي أَنْ أُعَلِّمَكُمْ مَا جَهِلْتُمْ مِمَّا عَلَّمَنِي يَوْمِي هَذَا: كُلُّ مَالٍ نَحَلْتُهُ عَبْدًا حَلاَلٌ، وَإِنِّي خَلَقْتُ عِبَادِى حُنَفَاءَ كُلَّهُمْ وَإِنَّهُمْ أَتَتْهُمُ الشَّيَاطِيْنُ فَاجْتَالَتْهُمْ عَنْ دِيْنِهِمْ وَحَرَّمَتْ عَلَيْهِمْ مَا احْلَلْتُ لَهُمْ وَأَمَرَتْهُمْ أَنْ يُشْرِكُوا بِي مَا لَمْ أُنَزِّلْ بِهِ سُلْطَانًا، وَإِنَّ اللهَ نَظَرَ إِلَى أَهْلِ الأَرْضِ فَمَقَتَهُمْ عَرَبَهُمْ وَعَجَمَهُمْ إِلاَّ بَقَايَا مِنْ أَهْلِ الْكِتَابِ، وَقَالَ إِنَّمَا بَعَثْتُكَ لأَبْتَلِيَكَ وَابْتَلِيَ بِكَ وَأَنْزَلْتُ عَلَيْكَ كِتَابًا لاَ يَغْسِلُهُ الْمَاءُ تَقْرَؤُهُ نَائِمًا وَيَقْظَانِ، وَإِنَّ اللهَ أَمَرَنِي أَنْ أُحَرِّقَ قُرَيْشًا، فَقُلْتُ: رَبِّ إِذًا يَثْلَغُوْا رَأْسِي فَيَدعُوْهُ خُبْزَةً قَالَ: اسْتَخْرِجْهُمْ كَمَا اسْتَخْرَجُوكَ وَاغْزُهُمْ نُغْزِكَ وَأَنْفِقْ فَسَنُنْفِقُ

عَلَيْكَ وَابْعَثْ جَيْشًا نَبْعَثْ خَمْسَةً مِثْلَهُ، وَقَاتِلْ بِمَنْ أَطَاعَكَ مِنْ عَصَاكَ، قَالَ: وَأَهْلُ الْجَنَّةِ ثَلاَثَةٌ: ذُوْ سُلْطَانٍ مُقْسِطٌ مُتَصَدِّقٌ مُوَفَّقٌ وَرَجُلٌ رَحِيْمٌ رَقِيْقُ الْقَلْبِ لِكُلِّ ذِي قُرْبَى وَمُسْلِمٍ وَعَفِيْفٌ مُتَعَفِّفٌ ذُوْ عِيَالٍ. قَالَ وَأَهْلُ النَّارِ خَمْسَةٌ: اَلضَّعِيْفُ الَّذِي لاَ زَبَرَ لَهُ الَّذِيْنَ هُمْ فِيْكُمْ تَبَعًا لاَ يَتْبَعُوْنَ أَهْلاً وَلاَ مَالاً، وَالْخَائِنُ الَّذِي لاَيَخْفَى لَهُ طَمَعٌ وَإِنْ دَقَّ إِلاَّ خَانَهُ، وَرَجُلٌ لاَ يُصْبِحُ وَلاَ يُمْسِي إِلاَّ وَهُوَ يُخَادِعُكَ عَنْ أَهْلِكَ وَمَالِكَ» وَذَكَرَ الْبُخْلَ أَوْ الْكَذِبَ «وَالشِّنْظِيْرُ الْفَحَّاشُ». «حديث صحيح» [رواه مسلم]

Some attributes of the Inhabitants of Paradise and Hell

35) A'Iyâd bin Himâr Al-Mujashi'i narrated that one day Allâh's Messenger صلى الله عليه وسلم said in his speech: Behold! Indeed Allâh has commanded me to inform you of what you are unfamiliar with; and what He has taught me today: Every wealth, I have conferred upon a slave is lawful. Indeed I have created My slaves being true in Faith; but the satans approached them and turned them away from their religion and what had been permissible declared as forbidden for them. Further the satans ordered them to make partners with me for which I have revealed no evidence. Verily, Allâh looked at the people on earth and hated both Arabs and non-Arabs - except a few people of the Scripture. Allâh added: I have sent you as a Prophet to the people so that I may test you and test the believers through you and revealed to you a book that water cannot erase. So you should read it while asleep and awake. The

Prophet صلى الله عليه وسلم said: Indeed Allâh has ordered me to burn (the disbelievers of) Quraish (the Prophet's tribe of Makkah). So I said: O Lord! They would crush my head like bread. Allâh said: Drive them out as they drove you out of your city. Fight them, We shall support you. Spend (money in the cause of Allâh), We will spend on you. Send an army, We will send five like that. Fight with your followers against those who deny you. He said: The inhabitants of Paradise are three kinds of people: First is a powerful, just, almsgiver, and a successful man. second is a kind, tender-hearted man towards every relative and Muslim. Third is a decent father to many children. He also said: Dwellers of Hell are of five types: First is a weak-follower man who has no sense to avoid the evil or work for family or wealth. Second is a dishonest man whose greed is well-known to people, even for minor things. Third is a man who will betray you about your family and wealth at both the ends of the day. He also mentioned a miser or a liar and a person who uses bad words.

(This *Hadîth* is sound and reported by Muslim).

In this *Hadith* the Prophet صلى الله عليه وسلم said that Allah عز وجل did not like the Arabs and non-Arabs except a few remnants of the peoples of the Books. This is meant for the period before the Message of Muhammad صلى الله عليه وسلم , but after the Message the previous Books were rendered invalid by the Noble Qur'ân, and the peoples of the Books (Christians and Jews) should have believed in Prophet Muhammad. Otherwise their belief in the invalidated and superceded Books will not be accepted by Allah عز وجل unlike what many people would think.

****

(٣٦) عَنْ أَبِي هُرَيْرَةَ رَضِيَ اللهُ عَنْهُ قَالَ: قَالَ النَّبِيُّ ﷺ:
«تَحَاجَّتِ الجَنَّةُ وَالنَّارُ فَقَالَتِ النَّارُ: أُوْثِرْتُ بِالْمُتَكَبِّرِيْنَ
وَالْمُتَجَبِّرِيْنَ، وَقَالَتِ الجَنَّةُ: مَالِيَ لاَ يَدْخُلُنِي إِلاَّ ضُعَفَاءُ

النَّاسِ وَسَقَطُهُمْ قَالَ اللهُ تَبَارَكَ وَتَعَالَى لِلْجَنَّةِ: أَنْتِ رَحْمَتِي أَرْحَمُ بِكِ مَنْ أَشَاءُ مِنْ عِبَادِي، وَقَالَ لِلنَّارِ إِنَّمَا أَنْتِ عَذَابٌ أُعَذِّبُ بِكِ مَنْ أَشَاءُ مِنْ عِبَادِي وَلِكُلِّ وَاحِدَةٍ مِنْهُمَا مَلْؤُهَا فَأَمَّا النَّارُ فَلاَ تَمْتَلِيءُ حَتَّى يَضَعَ رِجْلَهُ فَتَقُوْلُ قَطْ قَطْ قَطْ فَهُنَالِكَ تَمْتَلِيءُ وَيُزْوى بَعْضُهَا إِلَى بَعْضٍ وَلاَ يَظْلِمُ اللهُ عَزَّ وَجَلَّ مِنْ خَلْقِهِ أَحَدًا، وَأَمَّا الْجَنَّةُ فَإِنَّ اللهَ عَزَّ وَجَلَّ يُنْشِيءُ لَهَا خَلْقًا».

«حديث صحيح» [رواه البخاري ومسلم]

36) Narrated Abû Huraira رضى الله عنه: The Prophet صلى الله عليه وسلم said: Once Paradise and Hell argued with one another. Hell said: I have been given preference by the oppressors and tyrants. Paradise said: What is the matter with me that only weak and humble people enter me. Allâh عز وجل said to the Paradise: You are My mercy. I will bestow mercy through you on whom I wish from among My slaves. And He said to Hell: Rather you are My torment. I will torment by you whom I wish from among My slaves. The Prophet صلى الله عليه وسلم added: Each of them will take its capacity. As for Hell, it will not be filled until Allah puts down His glorified foot in it. Then it will say: Enough! Enough! Enough! at that time all its parts will be filled up. Allâh will not treat unjustly any one of His creation. As regards Paradise, Allâh will create other creations to fill it. (Being All-Merciful)

(This *Hadîth* is sound and reported by Bukhâri and Muslim).

On Doomsday, Allah عز وجل fills Hell by putting His Foot (a foot that suits his Glory and no human brain can perceive). As for Paradise he fills it by a new creation. This *Hadith* reveals that the mercy of Allah supercedes His anger, as He will not fill Paradise, too, by putting His Foot.

(٣٧) عَنْ أَنَسٍ رَضِيَ اللهُ عَنْهُ أَنَّ رَسُولَ اللهِ ﷺ قَالَ: «يُؤْتَى بِأَشَدِّ النَّاسِ كَانَ بَلَاءً فِي الدُّنْيَا مِنْ أَهْلِ الْجَنَّةِ فَيَقُولُ: أَصْبِغُوهُ صِبْغَةً فِي الْجَنَّةِ فَيُصْبِغُونَهُ فِيهَا صِبْغَةً فَيَقُولُ اللهُ عَزَّ وَجَلَّ: يَاابْنَ آدَمَ هَلْ رَأَيْتَ بُؤْسًا قَطْ أَوْ شَيْئًا تَكْرَهُهُ؟ فَيَقُولُ: لَا وَعِزَّتِكَ مَا رَأَيْتُ شَيْئًا أَكْرَهُهُ قَطْ ثُمَّ يُؤْتَى بِأَنْعَمِ النَّاسِ كَانَ فِي الدُّنْيَا مِنْ أَهْلِ النَّارِ فَيَقُولُ: اصْبِغُوهُ فِيهَا صِبْغَةً فَيَقُولُ: يَاابْنَ آدَمَ هَلْ رَأَيْتَ خَيْرًا قَطْ». «حديث صحيح» [رواه مسند أحمد]

Worthlessness of this world

37) Narrated Anas رضى الله عنه that Allâh's Messenger صلى الله عليه وسلم said: One of the most miserable people in the world will be brought from among the people of Paradise. Allâh will say (to the angels): Dip him once in Paradise. So they will dip him once in it. Then Allâh عز وجل will ask him: Did you ever face any distress or a thing you hate. He would say: No, by Your Glory! Never did I face anything unpleasant. Then one of the most affluent people of the world will be brought from Hell. Allâh will command (the angels:) Dip him once in it. Then He will ask him: O son of Adam! Did you ever enjoy any comfort? (that is, a dip in Hell can make one forget the meaning of comfort).

(This *Hadîth* is sound and reported in *Musnad Ahmad*).

A person who led a life of ease and plenty in this world.

****

(٣٨) عَنْ أَبِي سَعِيدٍ الْخُدْرِيِّ رَضِيَ اللهُ عَنْهُ عَنِ النَّبِيِّ ﷺ

قال: «يَقُوْلُ اللهُ تَبَارَكَ وَتَعَالَى: يَاآدَمُ فَيَقُوْلُ لَبَّيْكَ وَسَعْدَيْكَ وَالْخَيْرُ فِي يَدَيْكَ فَيَقُوْلُ: أَخْرِجْ بَعْثَ النَّارِ قَالَ: وَمَا بَعْثُ النَّارِ؟ قَالَ: مِنْ كُلِّ أَلْفٍ تِسْعَمِائَةٍ وَتِسْعَةً وَتِسْعِيْنَ فَعِنْدَهُ يَشِيْبُ الصَّغِيْرُ ﴿وَتَضَعُ كُلُّ ذَاتِ حَمْلٍ حَمْلَهَا وَتَرَى النَّاسَ سُكَارَى وَمَا هُمْ بِسُكَارَى وَلَكِنَّ عَذَابَ اللهِ شَدِيْدٌ﴾ قَالُوا يَارَسُولَ اللهِ وَأَيُّنَا ذٰلِكَ الوَاحِدُ قَالَ: أَبْشِرُوْا فَإِنَّ مِنْكُمْ رَجُلاً وَمِنْ يَأْجُوجَ وَمَأْجُوجَ أَلْفٌ. ثُمَّ قَالَ: وَالَّذِي نَفْسِي بِيَدِهِ إِنِّي أَرْجُو أَنْ تَكُونُوا رُبُعَ أَهْلِ الْجَنَّةِ، فَكَبَّرْنَا فَقَالَ: أَرْجُو أَنْ تَكُونُوا ثُلُثَ أَهْلِ الْجَنَّةِ، فَكَبَّرْنَا فَقَالَ: أَرْجُو أَنْ تَكُونُوا نِصْفَ أَهْلِ الْجَنَّةِ، فَكَبَّرْنَا فَقَالَ: مَا أَنْتُمْ فِي النَّاسِ إِلاَّ كَالشَّعْرَةِ السَّوْدَاءِ فِي جِلْدِ ثَوْرٍ أَبْيَضَ أَوْ كَشَعْرَةٍ بَيْضَاءَ فِي جِلْدِ ثَوْرٍ أَسْوَدَ». «حديث صحيح» [رواه البخاري ومسلم]

Some Scenes of Resurrection

38) Narrated Abû Sa'îd Al-Khudri رضي الله عنه that the Prophet صلى الله عليه وسلم said: Allâh تبارك وتعالى will call: O Adam! He will say: I respond to Your Call; I am obedient of Your Orders; and goodness rests in Your Hand. Allâh will say: Bring forth the group for Hell. Adam will ask: Who are the people doomed to Hell? Allâh will say: They are nine hundred and ninety-nine out of every one thousand. The Prophet صلى الله عليه وسلم said: At this juncture every child would turn grey-haired and every pregnant would miscarry

due to the dread of the moment and you would see people as drunk while they would not actually be. The torment of Allâh would be grievous enough to make them so. Then the Companions asked: O Allâh's Messenger صلى الله عليه وسلم! Who would be that single person among us? He said: Be happy! When one is selected (for Paradise) from among you, one thousand from Gog and Magog would be sent to Hell. Then he said: By Him in Whose Hand is my soul! I hope you will constitute one-fourth of the inhabitants of Paradise. We exclaimed الله اكبر (Allâh is All-Great).He said: I anticipate you would be one-third of the people of Paradise. Again we shouted الله اكبر. He said: I expect you would be half of the people of Paradise. Again we exclaimed الله اكبر. He further said: Despite, You would be just like a black hair in the skin of a white ox or like a white hair in the skin of a black one (i.e. your number compared with the non-Muslims will be very small but in Paradise you will be the majority).

(This *Hadîth* is sound and reported by Bukhâri and Muslim).

The *Ummah* (nation) of Prophet Muhammad صلى الله عليه وسلم is the best of all nations. Though they are the last they will be the first to enter Paradise by virtue of the Grace of Allah عز وجل which will bestowed on him as the Most Honoured Prophet, and his nation.

****

(٣٩) عَنْ أَبِي هُرَيرَةَ رَضِيَ اللهُ عَنْهُ قَالَ: قَالُوا يَارَسُوْلَ اللهِ: هَلْ نَرَى رَبَّنَا يَوْمَ الْقِيَامَةِ؟ قَالَ: «هَلْ تُضَارُّوْنَ فِي رُؤْيَةِ الشَّمْسِ فِي الظَّهِيْرَةِ لَيْسَتْ فِي سَحَابَةٍ قَالُوْا: لاَ قَالَ: فَهَلْ تُضَارُّوْنَ فِي رُؤْيَةِ الْقَمَرِ لَيْلَةَ الْبَدْرِ لَيْسَ فِي سَحَابَةٍ؟ قَالُوا: لاَ قَالَ: فَوَ الَّذِي نَفْسِي بِيَدِهِ لاَ تُضَارُّوْنَ فِي رُؤْيَةِ رَبِّكُمْ إِلاَّ كَمَا

تُضَارُّوْنَ فِي رُؤْيَةِ أَحَدِهِمَا . قَالَ فَيَلْقَى الْعَبْدُ فَيَقُولُ أَيْ قُلْ أَلَمْ أُكْرِمْكَ وَأُسَوِّدْكَ وَأُزَوِّجْكَ وَأُسَخِّرْ لَكَ الخَيْلَ وَالإِبِلَ وَأَذَرْكَ تَرْأَسُ وَتَرْبَعْ؟ فَيَقُولُ: بَلَى قَالَ: فَيَقُولُ: أَفَظَنَنْتَ أَنَّكَ مُلاَقِيَّ؟ فَيَقُولُ: لاَ فَيَقُولُ: فَإِنِّي أَنْسَاكَ كَمَا نَسِيتَنِي ثُمَّ يَلْقَى الثَّانِيَ فَيَقُولُ أَيْ قُلْ أَلَمْ أُكْرِمْكَ وَأُسَوِّدْكَ وَأُزَوِّجْكَ وَأُسَخِّرْ لَكَ الخَيْلَ وَالإِبِلَ وَأَذَرْكَ تَرْأَسُ وَتَرْبَعْ؟ فَيَقُولُ: بَلَى أَيْ رَبِّ! قَالَ: فَيَقُولُ: أَفَظَنَنْتَ أَنَّكَ مُلاَقِيَّ؟ فَيَقُولُ لاَ فَيَقُولُ: فَإِنِّي أَنْسَاكَ كَمَا نَسِيتَنِي ثُمَّ يَلْقَى الثَّالِثَ فَيَقُوْلُ لَهُ مِثْلَ ذٰلِكَ فَيَقُوْلُ: يَارَبِّ آمَنْتُ بِكَ وَبِكِتَابِكَ وَبِرُسُلِكَ وَصَلَّيْتُ وَصُمْتُ وَتَصَدَّقْتُ وَيُثْنِي بِخَيْرٍ مَا اسْتَطَاعَ فَيَقُوْلُ هَاهُنَا إِذًا، قَالَ ثُمَّ يُقَالُ لَهُ: الآنَ نَبْعَثُ شَاهِدَنَا عَلَيْكَ وَيَتَفَكَّرُ فِي نَفْسِهِ مَنْ ذَا الَّذِي يَشْهَدُ عَلَيَّ فَيُخْتَمُ عَلَى فِيْهِ وَيُقَالُ لِفَخِذِهِ وَلَحْمِهِ وَعِظَامِهِ انْطِقِي فَتَنْطِقُ فَخِذُهُ وَلَحْمُهُ وَعِظَامُهُ بِعَمَلِهِ وَذَلِكَ لِيعذرَ مِنْ نَفْسِهِ وَذَلِكَ الْمُنَافِقُ وَذٰلِكَ الَّذِي يَسْخَطُ اللهُ عَلَيْهِ».

«حديث صحيح» [رواه مسلم وأبو داؤود]

39) Narrated Abû Huraira رضي الله عنه: Once the Companions of the Prophet صلى الله عليه وسلم asked him: O Allâh's Messenger! Will we be able to see our Lord on the Day of Resurrection? He said: Do you feel any difficulty in seeing the sun at noon when it is not cloudy. They said: No. He further said: Do you

feel any difficulty in seeing the moon at the night of full moon when there is no cloud. They said: No. Thereupon he said: By Him who holds my life! You will not face any difficulty in seeing Allah as much as seeing one of them. The Prophet صلى الله عليه وسلم added: Then Allâh would sit for judgment upon the slaves and would say: O so-and-so! Did I not honour you and make you a chief and provide you a spouse and subdue for you horses and camels and offered you an opportunity to rule over your subjects and take one-fourth of booty. The slave would say, Yes. The Prophet صلى الله عليه وسلم said: Allâh would say: Did you not think that you would meet me? He would say: No. Thereupon, Allâh would say: I overlook you today as you forgot me. Then the second person will be brought (for judgment). Allâh would say: O so-and-so! Did I not honour you and make you the chief and make you a pair and subdue for you horses and camels and offered you an opportunity to rule over your subjects and take one-fourth of booty. He would say: Yes, my Lord! Then he would say: Did you not think that you would meet Me. The slave would say: No. At this moment Allâh would say: Well, I overlook you today as you forgot Me. Then the third one would be brought for judgment. Allâh would ask him the same thing. At this, the slave would say: O my Lord! I believed in You and Your Book and Your Messengers. Also, I performed prayers, observed fast and gave charity. Then he would speak in good terms like this. Allâh would say: Well. The Prophet صلى الله عليه وسلم added: Then, it would be said to him: Now, we will bring our witnesses to you. Then man will think: Who will bear witness upon me. Then, his mouth would be sealed and it would be said to his thighs, flesh and bones: Speak. So his thighs, flesh and bones would bear witness to his deeds. This is because he will not be able to make any excuse for himself. He would be a hypocrite whom Allâh would be angry with.

(This *Hadîth* is sound and reported by Muslim and Abû Dâ'ud).

****

(٤٠) عَنْ أَنَسِ بْنِ مَالِكٍ رَضِيَ اللهُ عَنْهُ قَالَ: كُنَّا عِنْدَ رَسُولِ اللهِ ﷺ فَضَحِكَ فَقَالَ: «هَلْ تَدْرُوْنَ مِمَّا أَضْحَكُ؟ قَالَ: قُلْنَا: اللهُ وَرَسُوْلُهُ أَعْلَمُ قَالَ: مِنْ مُخَاطَبَةِ الْعَبْدِ رَبَّهُ يَقُولُ يَارَبِّ أَلَمْ تُجِرْنِي مِنَ الظُّلْمِ؟ قَالَ: يَقُولُ بَلَى قَالَ: فَيَقُولُ فَإِنِّي لاَ أُجِيْزُ عَلَى نَفْسِي إِلاَّ شَاهِدًا مِنِّي قَالَ: فَيَقُوْلُ كَفَى بِنَفْسِكَ الْيَوْمَ عَلَيْكَ شَهِيْدًا وَبِالْكِرَامِ الْكَاتِبِيْنَ شُهُوْدًا، قَالَ: فَيُخْتَمُ عَلَى فِيْهِ فَيُقَالُ لأَرْكَانِهِ انْطِقِي قَالَ: فَتَنْطِقُ بِأَعْمَالِهِ قَالَ: ثُمَّ يُخْلَى بَيْنَهُ وَبَيْنَ الْكَلاَمِ قَالَ فَيَقُولُ بُعْدًا لَكُنَّ وَسُحْقًا فَعَنْكُنَّ كُنْتُ أُنَاضِلُ». «حديث صحيح» [رواه مسلم]

40) Narrated Anas bin Mâlik رضى الله عنه: We were in the company of Allâh's Messenger صلى الله عليه وسلم when he laughed and said: Do you know why I laughed? The narrator said: We said: Allâh and His Messenger know best. Then the Prophet صلى الله عليه وسلم said: I laughed at the talk of the slave to his Lord on the Day of Resurrection as he would say: O my Lord! Have You not guaranteed me protection against injustice? The Prophet صلى الله عليه وسلم said: Allâh would say: Yes. The Prophet صلى الله عليه وسلم added: Then the slave would say: Today I do not allow any witness against me except a witness of my own self. Then the Prophet صلى الله عليه وسلم said: Allâh would say: Today only yourself and the noble recording angels would be witnesses to you. Then the Prophet صلى الله عليه وسلم said: Then his mouth would be sealed and it would be said to his limbs: Speak. The Prophet صلى الله عليه وسلم added: They would

speak of his deeds. He صلى الله عليه وسلم said: Then he would be made free to talk. The Prophet صلى الله عليه وسلم said: He would say to his limbs: Woe and curse be upon you. For only your sake I was contending.

This *Hadith* shows the controversial nature of man. Allah سبحانه و تعالى being All-Knower of this, will make man's own body parts witnesses for him.

****

(٤١) عَنْ أَبِي هُرَيرَةَ رَضِيَ اللهُ عَنْهُ قَالَ: سَمِعْتُ رَسُولَ اللهِ ﷺ يَقُولُ: «يَقْبِضُ اللهُ الأَرْضَ وَيَطْوِي السَّمَاوَاتِ بِيَمِينِهِ ثُمَّ يَقُولُ: أَنَا الْمَلِكُ أَيْنَ مُلُوكُ الأَرْضِ».

«حديث صحيح» [رواه البخاري ومسلم]

Statement of Allâh عز وجل: "All the earth is in His possession on the Day of Resurrection"

41) Narrated Abû Huraira رضى الله عنه: I heard Allâh's Messenger saying: Allâh would grasp the whole planet of the earth and roll it up on the Day of Resurrection and all the heavens will be in His Right Hand. Then He will say: I am the King. Where are the monarchs of the earth?

(This *Hadîth* is sound and reported by Bukhâri and Muslim).

According to Islamic creed Allah عز وجل is Unique in His Names and Attributes. These Attributes cannot be perceived by the human mind e.g. in this *Hadith* the Prophet صلى الله عليه وسلم said: Allah عز وجل will hold the earth and roll the heavens by His Right Hand. As we believe that Allah عز وجل is All-Mighty, All-Knower, All-Hearer and that His Powers are uncountable and beyond any measurement, we have to believe that He holds, on the Day of Resurrection, the earth and the heaven as mentioned by the Prophet صلى الله عليه وسلم .

****

(٤٢) عَنْ أَبِي هُرَيرَةَ رَضِيَ اللهُ عَنْهُ قَالَ: قَالَ رَسُولُ اللهِ ﷺ: «إِنَّ أَوَّلَ مَا يُسْأَلُ عَنْهُ يَوْمَ الْقِيامَةِ - يَعْنِي الْعَبْدُ - مِنَ النَّعِيمِ أَنْ يُقَالَ لَهُ أَلَمْ نُصِحَّ لَكَ جِسْمَكَ وَنُرْوِيكَ مِنَ الْمَاءِ الْبَارِدِ».

«حديث صحيح» [رواه الترمذي]

Question about the worldly pleasure on the Day of Resurrection

42) Narrated Abû Huraira رضى الله عنه: Allâh's Messenger صلى الله عليه وسلم said: First of the things a slave will be questioned about on the Day of Judgment will be the gifts of Allâh. It would bc said to him: Did we not give you a healthy body, and did we not saturate you with cold water.

(This *Hadîth* is sound and reported by Tirmidhi).

To appreciate such a drink, can you imaginc a healthy man when he is so thirsty then finds water!

****

(٤٣) عَنِ ابْنِ عَبَّاسٍ رَضِيَ اللهُ عَنْهُمَا قَالَ: قَالَتْ قُرَيْشٌ لِلنَّبِيِّ ﷺ: ادْعُ لَنَا رَبَّكَ أَنْ يَجْعَلَ لَنَا الصَّفَا ذَهَبًا وَنُؤْمِنُ بِكَ قَالَ: «وَتَفْعَلُونَ، قَالُوا: نَعَمْ قَالَ: فَدَعَا فَأَتَاهُ جِبْرِيْلُ فَقَالَ: إِنَّ رَبَّكَ عَزَّ وَجَلَّ يَقْرَأُ عَلَيْكَ السَّلَامَ وَيَقُولُ: إِنْ شِئْتَ أُصَبِّحُ لَهُمْ الصَّفَا ذَهَبًا فَمَنْ كَفَرَ بَعْدَ ذَلِكَ مِنْهُمْ عَذَّبْتُهُ عَذَابًا لاَ أُعَذِّبُهُ أَحَدًا مِنَ الْعَالَمِيْنَ، وَإِنْ شِئْتَ فَتَحْتُ لَهُمْ بَابَ التَّوْبَةِ وَالرَّحْمَةِ. قَالَ بَلْ بَابُ التَّوْبَةِ وَالرَّحْمَةِ».

«حديت صحيح» [رواه مسند أحمد]

Compassion of Allâh's Messenger صلى الله عليه وسلم on his *Ummah*

43) Narrated Ibn 'Abbâs رضى الله عنهما: The tribe of Quraish said to the Prophet صلى الله عليه وسلم: Supplicate your Lord that He transforms (the rocks of) Safa into gold. Then we would believe in you. He (the Prophet صلى الله عليه وسلم) asked: Really, will you? They said: Yes. He (the narrator said: So the Prophet صلى الله عليه وسلم) invoked Allah (to this effect). Then Jibrael came to him and said: Your Lord عز وجل conveys His greetings to you and says: If you wish, I shall transform Safa into gold but those who disbelieve after that will suffer a punishment so severe that nobody in the worlds would suffer, or if you wish, I can open for them the door of repentance and mercy. The Prophet صلى الله عليه وسلم) said: Rather, the door of repentance and mercy.

(This *Hadîth* is sound and reported in *Musand Ahmad*).

Prophet Muhammad صلى الله عليه وسلم being so kind and humane by the blessings of Allah عز وجل , used to invoke Allah عز وجل for his Companions. He also used to go to the Baqi' where most of his Companions had been buried in Al-Madina and ask Allah to make them rest in peace. He even did this at times very late at nights. What a kind-hearted Prophet he was

****

(٤٤) عَنْ عُبَادَةَ بْنِ الصَّامِتِ رَضِيَ اللهُ عَنْهُ قَالَ : فَقَدَ النَّبِيَّ ﷺ يَوْمًا أَصْحَابُهُ وَكَانُوا إِذَا نَزَلُوْا أَنْزَلُوْهُ أَوْسَطَهُمْ فَفَزِعُوا وَظَنُّوا أَنَّ اللهَ تَبَارَكَ وَتَعَالَى اخْتَارَ لَهُ أَصْحَابًا غَيْرَهُمْ فَإِذَا هُمْ بِخَيَالِ النَّبِيِّ ﷺ فَكَبَّرُوْا حِيْنَ رَأَوْهُ وَقَالُوا : يَارَسُولَ اللهِ أَشْفَقْنَا أَنْ يَكُوْنَ اللهُ تَبَارَكَ وَتَعَالَى اخْتَارَ لَكَ أَصْحَابًا غَيْرَنَا فَقَالَ رَسُوْلُ

اللهِ ﷺ: «لاَ بَلْ أَنْتُمْ أَصْحَابِي فِي الدُّنْيَا وَالآخِرَةِ إِنَّ اللهَ تَعَالَى أَيْقَظَنِي فَقَالَ: يَامُحَمَّدُ إِنِّي لَمْ أَبْعَثْ نَبِيًّا وَلاَ رَسُوْلاً إِلاَّ وَقَدْ سَأَلَنِي مَسْأَلَةً أَعْطَيْتُهَا إِيَّاهُ فَاسْأَلْ يَامُحَمَّدُ تُعْطَ فَقُلْتُ مَسْأَلَتِي شَفَاعَةٌ لأُمَّتِي يَوْمَ الْقِيَامَةِ، فَقَالَ أَبُو بَكْرٍ: يَارَسُوْلَ اللهِ وَمَا الشَّفَاعَةُ؟ قَالَ: أَقُولُ يَاربِّ شَفَاعَتِي الَّتِي اخْتَبَأْتُ عِنْدَكَ فَيَقُوْلُ الرَّبُّ تَبَارَكَ وَتَعَالَى: نَعَمْ فَيُخْرِجُ رَبِّي تَبَارَكَ وَتَعَالَى بَقِيَّةَ أُمَّتِي مِنَ النَّارِ فَيَنْبِذُهُمْ فِي الجَنَّةِ». «حديث حسن» [رواه مسند أحمد]

44) Narrated Ubâda bin As-Sâmit رضي الله عنه: One day the Companions did not find the Prophet صلى الله عليه وسلم among them. (Normally) when they camped, they would lodge him in the middle (of them). They were anxious and thinking that Allah might have selected some other Companions for him. Suddenly, they saw him coming towards them and exclaimed الله اكبر (Allâh is All-Great) and they said: O Allâh's Messenger! We feared that Allâh تبارك وتعالى must have selected for you some Companions other than ourselves. Allâh's Messenger صلى الله عليه وسلم said: No. Rather you are my companions in this world and the Hereafter. Indeed Allâh, the Almighty, awakened me and said: O Muhammad! Verily, I have neither sent any Prophet nor a Messenger without a wish to which I respond and that I now grant you too. So O Muhammad! You should also ask Me something which would be given to you. The Prophet صلى الله عليه وسلم said: My wish is an intercession for my followers on the Day of Resurrection., Abû Bakr asked: O Allâh's Messenger! What is intercession? He (the Prophet) صلى الله عليه وسلم said: I will say: O Lord! My intercession is the pledge I have kept with

you. Thereupon, the Lord تبارك وتعالى will say: Yes. Then my Lord will take out the rest of my followers from Hell and admit them into Paradise.

(This *Hadîth* is sound and reported in *Musnad Ahmad*).

****

(٤٥) عَنْ أَبِي هُرَيْرَةَ رَضِيَ اللهُ عَنْهُ أَنَّهُ عَادَ مَرِيضًا مِنْ وَعْكٍ، وَكَانَ مَعَ أَبِي هُرَيْرَةَ رَسُولُ اللهِ ﷺ فَقَالَ لَهُ رَسُولُ اللهِ ﷺ: «أَبْشِرْ إِنَّ اللهَ عَزَّ وَجَلَّ يَقُوْلُ: نَارِي أُسَلِّطُهَا عَلَى عَبْدِي الْمُؤْمِنِ فِي الدُّنْيَا لِتَكُوْنَ حَظَّهُ مِنَ النَّارِ فِي الآخِرَةِ».

«حديث حسن» [رواه أحمد وابن ماجه والترمذي]

Fever and other diseases lessen sins

45) Narrated Abû Huraira رضى الله عنه that with Allâh Messenger صلى الله عليه وسلم once he visited a patient suffering from fever. Allâh's Messenger صلى الله عليه وسلم said to the patient: Rejoice with the good news that Allâh عزوجل says: I shall afflict My faithful slave in the world with My fire (fever) so that he may be saved from his share of fire in the Hereafter.

(This *Hadîth* is good and reported by Ahmad in his *Musnad*, Ibn Mâjah and Tirmidhi).

A faithful slave who suffers from fever and other diseases in the world will be accordingly forgiven some sins in the Hereafter.

****

(٤٦) عَنْ عُقْبَةَ بْنِ عَامِرٍ رَضِيَ اللهُ عَنْهُ قَالَ: قَالَ النَّبِيُّ ﷺ: «لَيْسَ مِنْ عَمَلِ يَوْمٍ إِلاَّ وَهُوَ يُخْتَمُ عَلَيْهِ فَإِذَا مَرِضَ الْمُؤْمِنُ

قَالَتِ الْمَلاَئِكَةُ : يَارَبَّنَا عَبْدُكَ فُلاَنٌ قَدْ حَبَسْتَهُ فَيَقُوْلُ الرَّبُّ عَزَّ وَجَلَّ : اخْتِمُوْا لَهُ عَلَى مِثْلِ عَمَلِهِ حَتَّى يَبْرَأَ أَوْ يَمُوْتَ» .

«حديث صحيح» [رواه مسند أحمد]

When a slave falls sick, reward will be recorded for him according to what he was doing in the state of health

(When a slave is sick, he gets reward to his credit according to the deeds he was doing when he was healthy)

46) Narrated Uqba bin Aamir رضى الله عنه: The Prophet صلى الله عليه وسلم said: Every deed of a day is sealed up. When a believer falls ill, the angels say: O our Lord! Your slave so-and-so has fallen ill. The Lord عزوجل says: Note down to his credit the same deeds, he was doing before illness, until he heals up or dies.

(This *Hadîth* is sound and reported by Ahmad in his *Musnad*).

****

(٤٧) عَنْ أَنَسِ بْنِ مَالِكٍ رَضِيَ اللهُ عَنْهُ قَالَ : سَمِعْتُ النَّبِيَّ ﷺ يَقُولُ : «إِنَّ اللهَ عَزَّ وَجَلَّ قَالَ : إِذَا ابْتَلَيْتُ عَبْدِي بِحَبِيْبَتَيْهِ فَصَبَرَ عَوَّضْتُهُ مِنْهُمَا الْجَنَّةَ» . «حديث صحيح» [رواه البخاري]

One who is deprived of his eyesight and remains patient, Allâh's reward for him will be Paradise

47) Narrated Anas bin Mâlik رضى الله عنه: I heard the Prophet صلى الله عليه وسلم saying: Allâh said: If I deprive My slave of his two beloved things (i.e. his eyes) and he remains patient, I

will let him enter Paradise in compensation for them.

(This *Hadîth* is sound and reported by Bukhâri).

The Mercy of Allah عز وجل is unlimited. Loss of sight in this world is reckoned and the compensation in the Hereafter is Paradise.

****

(٤٨) عَنْ جُنْدُبٍ بْنِ عَبْدِ اللهِ رَضِيَ اللهُ عَنْهُ قَالَ: قَالَ رَسُولُ اللهِ ﷺ: «كَانَ فِيمَنْ كَانَ قَبْلَكُمْ رَجُلٌ بِهِ جُرْحٌ فَجَزِعَ فَأَخَذَ سِكِّيْنًا فَحَزَّ بِهَا يَدَهُ فَمَا رَقَأَ الدَّمُ حَتَّى مَاتَ قَالَ اللهُ تَعَالَى: بَادَرَنِي عَبْدِي بِنَفْسِهِ حَرَّمْتُ عَلَيْهِ الْجَنَّةَ».

«حديث صحيح» [رواه البخاري ومسلم]

Intimidation against committing suicide

48) Narrated Jundub bin 'Abdullâh رضي الله عنه: Allâh's Messenger صلى الله عليه وسلم said: Among the nations before you was a man who got a wound and was impatient. He took a knife and cut his hand. Blood did not cease to flow until he died. Allâh the Exalted said: My slave hurried to bring death upon himself. So I will not allow him to enter Paradise.

(This *Hadîth* is sound and reported by Bukhâri and Muslim).

Suicide is prohibited in Islam. You may say 'I am free to kill myself'. No, you do not have this right as you are a slave of Allah. Your death is not to be caused by yourself. Nor should you kill somebody else. Both suicide and homicide are unacceptable in Islam. Any murderer is a big sinner who should also be killed, as a penalty in this world and Hell is what he deserves in the Hereafter. Even he who commits suicide will be punished by Hell.

****

(٤٩) عَنْ عَبْدِ اللهِ بْنِ مَسْعُودٍ رَضِيَ اللهُ عَنْهُ عَنِ النَّبِيِّ ﷺ قَالَ: «يَجِيْءُ الرَّجُلُ آخِذًا بِيَدِ الرَّجُلِ فَيَقُوْلُ: يَارَبِّ هَذَا قَتَلَنِي فَيَقُوْلُ اللهُ لَهُ: لِمَ قَتَلْتَهُ فَيَقُوْلُ: قَتَلْتُهُ لِتَكُوْنَ العِزَّةُ لَكَ فَيَقُوْلُ: فَإِنَّهَا لِي، وَيَجِيْءُ الرَّجُلُ آخِذًا بِيَدِ الرَّجُلِ فَيَقُوْلُ: إِنَّ هَذَا قَتَلَنِي فَيَقُوْلُ اللهُ لَهُ: لِمَ قَتَلْتَهُ فَيَقُوْلُ: لِتَكُوْنَ الْعِزَّةُ لِفُلَانٍ فَيَقُوْلُ: إِنَّهَا لَيْسَتْ لِفُلَانٍ فَيَبُوءَ بِإِثْمِهِ».

«حديث صحيح لغيره» [رواه النسائي]

Sin of the one who murders unjustly

49) Narrated ‘Abdullâh bin Mas‘ûd رضى الله عنه on the authority of the Prophet صلى الله عليه وسلم: (On the Day of Judgment) a man will come holding the hand of another man and say: O Lord! It is he who killed me. Allâh will say: Why did you kill him? He will say: I killed him so that glory may be established for you. Allâh will say: Indeed it. Then another will come taking hold of another fellow's hand and say: It is he who killed me. Allâh will ask him: Why did you kill him? He will say: I killed him so that glory may be established for so-and-so person. Allâh will say: Indeed glory is not his. (So the killer will bear the sin).

(This *Hadîth* is sound and reported by Nasa'i).

****

(٥٠) عَنْ أَبِي هُرَيرَةَ رَضِيَ اللهُ عَنْهُ قَالَ: قَالَ النَّبِيُّ ﷺ: «يَقُولُ اللهُ تَعَالَى: أَنَا عِنْدَ ظَنِّ عَبْدِي بِي وَأَنَا مَعَهُ إِذَا ذَكَرَنِي فَإِنْ ذَكَرَنِي فِي نَفْسِهِ ذَكَرْتُهُ فِي نَفْسِي، وَإِنْ ذَكَرَنِي فِي مَلأٍ

ذَكَرْتُهُ فِي مَلأٍ خَيْرٍ مِنْهُمْ وَإِنْ تَقَرَّبَ إِلَيَّ شِبْرًا تَقَرَّبْتُ إِلَيْهِ ذِرَاعًا ، وَإِنْ تَقَرَّبَ إِلَيَّ ذِرَاعًا تَقَرَّبْتُ إِلَيْهِ بَاعًا وَإِنْ أَتَانِي يَمْشِي أَتَيْتُهُ هَرْوَلَةً» . «حديث صحيح» [رواه البخاري ومسلم]

Superiority of *Dhikr* (remembrance) and becoming close to Allâh by way of righteous deeds and good faith in Him

50) Narrated Abû Huraira رضى الله عنه: The Prophet صلى الله عليه وسلم said: Allâh تعالى says: I am in accordance with the thoughts of My slave about Me; and I am with him, when he remembers Me. If he remembers Me in his heart, I also remember him in My heart. If he remembers Me in a group, I remember him in a better group (i.e. angels). If he draws near Me by the span of a palm, I draw near him by a cubit. If he draws near Me by a cubit, I draw near him by the space covered by two hands. If he walks towards Me, I go to him running.

(This *Hadîth* is sound and reported by Bukhâri and Muslim).

****

(٥١) عَنْ أَبِي هُرَيْرَةَ رَضِيَ اللهُ عَنْهُ عَنِ النَّبِيِّ ﷺ قَالَ : «إِنَّ اللهَ عَزَّ وَجَلَّ يَقُوْلُ أَنَا مَعَ عَبْدِى إِذَا هُوَ ذَكَرَنِي وَتَحَرَّكَتْ بِي شَفَتَاهُ» . «حديث صحيح» [رواه مسند أحمد]

51) Narrated Abû Huraira رضى الله عنه that the Prophet صلى الله عليه وسلم stated: Allâh عز وجل observed: I am with My slave when he remembers me and moves his lips (with remembrance).

(This *Hadîth* is sound and reported in *Musnad*

Ahmad).

Repetition of Allah's chants and His virtues for example: *Subhân Allah, Al-Hamdu Lillah, and Allahu Akbar* سبحان الله، الحمد لله، الله اكبر .

****

(٥٢) عَنْ أَبِي هُرَيْرَةَ وَأَبِي سَعِيْدٍ أَنَّهُمَا شَهِدَا عَلَى رَسُوْلِ اللهِ ﷺ «إِذَا قَالَ العَبْدُ لاَ إِلٰهَ إِلاَّ اللهُ وَاللهُ أَكْبَرُ قَالَ: يَقُوْلُ اللهُ عَزَّ وَجَلَّ: صَدَقَ عَبْدِي لاَ إِلٰهَ إِلاَّ أَنَا وَأَنَا أَكْبَرُ، وَإِذَا قَالَ العَبْدُ لاَ إِلٰهَ إِلاَّ اللَّهُ وَحْدَهُ قَالَ: صَدقَ عَبْدِي لاَ إِلٰهَ إِلاَّ أَنَا وَحْدِي، وَإِذَا قَالَ: لاَ إِلٰهَ إِلاَّ اللهُ لاَشَرِيْكَ لَهُ قَالَ: صَدَقَ عَبْدِي لاَ إِلٰهَ إِلاَّ أَنَا وَلاَ شَرِيْكَ لِي، وَإِذَا قَالَ: لاَ إِلٰهَ إِلاَّ اللهُ لَهُ الْمُلْكُ وَلَهُ الْحَمْدُ قَالَ صَدَقَ عَبْدِي لاَ إِلٰهَ إِلاَّ أَنَا لِيَ المُلْكُ وَلِيَ الحَمْدُ وَإِذَا قَالَ لاَ إِلٰهَ إِلاَّ اللهُ وَلاَ حَوْلَ وَلاَ قُوَّةَ إِلاَّ بِاللهِ قَالَ: صَدَقَ عَبْدِي لاَ إِلٰهَ إِلاَّ أَنَا وَلاَ حَوْلَ وَلاَ قُوَّةَ إِلاَّ بِي».

«حديث صحيح» [رواه ابن ماجه والترمذي وابن حبان]

52) (One day) Abû Huraira and Abû Sa'îd رضى الله عنهما were sitting with Allâh's Messenger صلى الله عليه وسلم who said: When a slave says: لا اله الا الله والله اكبر i.e., There is no God but Allâh and Allâh is the Most-Great. Allâh remarks: My slave has spoken the truth. Indeed, there is no god except Me and I am All-Great. When he says: لا اله الا الله i.e., There is no God but Allâh and He is the only One. Allâh remarks: My slave has spoken the truth. Indeed, there is no God except Me and I am the One. When he says: لا اله الا الله وحده لا شريك له i.e., There is no God but Allâh and there is no

associate with Him. Allâh remarks: My slave has spoken the truth. There is no God except Me and I have no partner. When he says: لا اله الا الله له الملك وله الحمد i.e., There is no God but Allâh. To Him belongs the sovereignty and to Him is due all praise. Allâh remarks: My slave has spoken the truth. There is no God except Me. To Me belongs the kingdom and to Me is due all praise. When he says: لا اله الا الله ولاحول ولا قوة الا بالله i.e., There is no God but Allâh and there is no power or might except with Him. Allâh remarks: My slave has spoken the truth. There is no God except Me and the power and might belong to Me.

(Its chain of narratirs is sound and reported by Ibn Mâjah, Tirmidhi and Ibn Hibbân).

In Islam, remembrance of Allah عز وجل is very much recommended, anywhere, any time, and in any condition—Such words: الله اكبر الحمد لله سبحان الله are very easy to pronounce but very valuable in reward.

****

(٥٣) عَنْ أَبِي هُرَيرَةَ رَضِيَ اللهُ عَنْهُ قَالَ: قَالَ رَسُولُ اللهِ ﷺ: «إِنَّ للهِ مَلاَئِكَةً يَطُوفُوْنَ فِي الطُّرُقِ يَلْتَمِسُوْنَ أَهْلَ الذِّكْرِ، فَإِذَا وَجَدُوْا قَوْمًا يَذْكُرُوْنَ اللَّهَ تَنَادَوْا هَلُمُّوا إِلَى حَاجَتِكُمْ قَالَ: فَيَحُفُّوْنَهُمْ بِأَجْنِحَتِهِمْ إِلَى السَّمَاءِ الدُّنْيَا قَالَ: فَيَسْأَلُهُمْ رَبُّهُمْ عَزَّ وَجَلَّ - وَهُوَ أَعْلَمُ مِنْهُمْ - مَا يَقُوْلُ عِبَادِي؟ قَالَ: تَقُوْلُ: يُسَبِّحُوْنَكَ وَيُكَبِّرُوْنَكَ وَيَحْمَدُوْنَكَ وَيُمَجِّدُوْنَكَ قَالَ: فَيَقُوْلُ: هَلْ رَأَوْنِي؟ قَالَ: فَيَقُولُوْنَ لاَ وَاللَّهِ مَا رَأَوْكَ قَالَ: فَيَقُوْلُ: كَيْفَ لَوْ رَأَوْنِي؟ قَالَ: يَقُوْلُونَ: لَوْ رَأَوْكَ كَانُوا أَشَدَّ

لَكَ عِبَادَةً وَأَشَدَّ لَكَ تَمْجِيْدًا وَأَكْثَرَ تَسْبِيْحًا قَالَ: يَقُوْلُ: فَمَا يَسْأَلُوْنِي؟ قَالُوا: يَسْأَلُوْنَكَ الجَنَّةَ قَالَ: يَقُوْلُ: وَهَلْ رَأَوْهَا؟ قَالَ: يَقُوْلُوْنَ: لاَ وَاللَّهِ يَارَبِّ مَا رَأَوْهَا قَالَ: فَيَقُوْلُ: فَكَيْفَ لَوْ أَنَّهُمْ رَأَوْهَا؟ قَالَ: يَقُوْلُونَ لَوْ أَنَّهُمْ رَأَوْهَا كَانُوْا أَشَدَّ عَلَيْهَا حِرْصًا وَأَشَدَّ لَهَا طَلَبًا وَأَعْظَمَ فِيْهَا رَغْبَةً قَالَ: فَمِمَّ يَتَعَوَّذُوْنَ؟ قَالَ: يَقُوْلُونَ مِنَ النَّارِ قَالَ: يَقُوْلُ: وَهَلْ رَأَوْهَا؟ قَالَ: فَيَقُوْلُونَ لاَ وَاللَّهِ يَارَبِّ مَا رَأَوْهَا قَالَ: يَقُوْلُ فَكَيْفَ لَوْ رَأَوْهَا؟ قَالَ: يَقُوْلُونَ لَوْ رَأَوْهَا كَانَ أَشَدَّ مِنْهَا فِرَارًا وَأَشَدَّ لَهَا مَخَافَةً قَالَ: فَيَقُوْلُ: فَأُشْهِدُكُمْ أَنِّي قَدْ غَفَرْتُ لَهُمْ قَالَ: يَقُوْلُ مَلَكٌ مِنَ الْمَلاَئِكَةِ فِيْهِمْ فُلاَنٌ لَيْسَ مِنْهُمْ إِنَّمَا جَاءَ لِحَاجَةٍ قَالَ: هُمُ الْجُلَسَاءُ لاَ يَشْقَى بِهِمْ جَلِيْسُهُمْ».

«حديث صحيح» [رواه البخاري ومسلم]

Superiority of the company of pious people

53) Narrated Abû Huraira رضي الله عنه: Allâh's Messenger صلى الله عليه وسلم said: Allâh has some angels who roam about the streets in search of people mentioning Allâh's Names. When they find such a gathering, they call one another saying: Come to the object of your pursuit. The Prophet صلى الله عليه وسلم added: The angels surround them with their wings up to the lowest heaven (sky of the world). He further added: (When the people in the gathering disperse, the angels ascend to the heaven). Their Lord, who knows best about the people, asks them: What do my slaves say?

The angels reply: They were glorifying You (by repeating the words "Allah is the All-Glorified" سبحان الله), exalting You (by repeating the words "Allah is All-Great" الله اكبر), praising You (by repeating the words "All praise be to Allah" الحمد لله), and dignifying You. He asks them: Have they seen Me? The angels reply: No, by Allâh. O Lord! They haven't seen You (at all). He asks: How would it be if they saw Me? The angels reply: If they saw You, they would worship You more devotedly, dignify You more fervently and exalt You more sincerely. Then Allâh asks them: What do they ask Me? The angels reply: They ask You Paradise. He asks them: Have they seen it? The angels reply: No, by Allâh, they have not seen it. He asks: How would it be, if they saw it? The angels reply: If they saw it, they would crave for it eagerly, seek after it vigorously and desire it ardently. He asks: From what do they seek My protection? The angels reply: (They seek your protection) from Hell. He asks: Have they seen it? The angels reply: No, by Allâh, O Lord! They haven't see it (at all). He asks: How would it be, if they saw it. The angels reply: If they saw it, they would fear it extremely and flee from it hastily. Then Allâh says (to the angels): I make you witness that I have forgiven them. Allâh's Messenger صلى الله عليه وسلم added: One of the angels would say: O Lord! among them was so-and-so (a much sinning slave) who was not actually included in the gathering but he happened to came there for some need (and sat down with them). Allâh would remark: Anyhow, they were all sitting together, so their companion will not be reduced to misery (i.e. they were sitting together and glorifying Allâh, so he who sits with them will not suffer but get forgiveness as a reward for his association with the people remembering Allâh).

(This *Hadîth* is sound and reported by Bukhâri and Muslim).

****

(٥٤) عَنْ أَبِي هُرَيرَةَ رَضِيَ اللهُ عَنْهُ قَالَ: سَمِعْتُ النَّبِيَّ ﷺ قَالَ: «إِنَّ عَبْدًا أَصَابَ ذَنْبًا ـ وَرُبَّمَا قَالَ أَذْنَبَ ذَنْبًا ـ فَقَالَ: رَبِّ أَذْنَبْتُ ذَنْبًا وَرُبَّمَا قَالَ أَصَبْتُ ـ فَاغْفِرْ فَقَالَ رَبُّهُ أَعَلِمَ عَبْدِي أَنَّ لَهُ رَبًّا يَغْفِرُ الذَّنْبَ وَيَأْخُذُ بِهِ؟ غَفَرْتُ لِعَبْدِي ثُمَّ مَكَثَ مَا شَاءَ اللَّهُ ثُمَّ أَصَابَ ذَنْبًا أَوْ أَذْنَبَ ذَنْبًا فَقَالَ رَبِّ أَذْنَبْتُ ـ أَوْ أَصَبْتُ ـ آخَرَ فَاغْفِرْهُ فَقَالَ: أَعَلِمَ عَبْدِي أَنَّ لَهُ رَبًّا يَغْفِرُ الذَّنْبَ وَيَأْخُذُ بِهِ؟ غَفَرْتُ لِعَبْدِي ثُمَّ مَكَثَ مَا شَاءَ اللَّهُ ثُمَّ أَذْنَبَ ذَنْبًا وَرُبَّمَا قَالَ أَصَابَ ذَنْبًا ـ فَقَالَ رَبِّ أَصَبْتُ ـ أَوْ أَذْنَبْتُ ـ آخَرَ فَاغْفِرْهُ لِي فَقَالَ: أَعَلِمَ عَبْدَي أَنَّ لَهُ رَبًّا يَغْفِرُ الذَّنْبَ وَيَأْخُذُ بِهِ؟ غَفَرْتُ لِعَبْدِي ثَلاَثًا فَلْيَعْمَلْ مَا شَاءَ».

«حديث صحيح» [رواه البخاري ومسلم]

Continuous inducement for repentance and seeking Allâh's forgiveness

54) Narrated Abû Huraira رضي الله عنه: I heard Prophet Muhammad صلى الله عليه وسلم saying that: a sin was committed by one of the slaves or may be he said, that: one of the slaves committed a sin. He said: O my Lord! I have committed a sin, or he said, a sin was committed by me. So please forgive me. His Lord would say: Does My slave know that he has a Lord who can forgive him and (if He likes) can punish him. Anyhow, I have forgiven My slave.

No sooner does the time elapse as much as Allâh wishes, than is another sin committed by him or he commits another sin. He says: O my Lord! I have committed a sin, or a sin was committed by me. So please forgive it. Allâh will observe: Does My slave know that he has a Lord who can forgive him and (if He likes) punish him too. Anyhow, I have forgiven him again. No sooner does the time elapse as much as Allâh wishes, than is another sin committed by him or he commits another sin. He says: O my Lord! I have committed another sin, or sometimes he says another sin is committed by me. So please forgive it. Allâh will remark: Does My slave know that he has a Lord who can forgive him and (if He likes) can punish him too. Anyhow, I have forgiven him for the third time. So let him do whatever he wishes.

(This *Hadîth* is sound and reported by Bukhâri and Muslim).

This is an example of Allah's mercy on His believers. If a believer happens to commit a sin, he should repent hoping for the forgiveness of Allah but, continuous pursuit of evils intentionally will not be fruitful in his favour because Allah has gifted every man with discretion to differentiate between good and evil. So one should be faithful to Allah and follow the example of Prophet Muhammad صلى الله عليه وسلم in all his deeds.

****

(٥٥) عَنْ أَبِي سَعِيْدٍ الخُدْرِيِّ رَضِيَ اللهُ عَنْهُ قَالَ: سَمِعْتُ رَسُولَ اللهِ ﷺ يقول: «إِنَّ إِبْلِيْسَ قَالَ لِرَبِّهِ: بِعِزَّتِكَ وَجَلَالِكَ لَا أَبْرَحُ أَغْوِي بَنِي آدَمَ مَا دَامَتِ الأَرْوَاحُ فِيْهِمْ فَقَالَ اللَّهُ: فَبِعِزَّتِي وَجَلَالِي لَا أَبْرَحُ أَغْفِرُ لَهُمْ مَا اسْتَغْفَرُوْنِي».

«حديث صحيح» [رواه مسند أحمد]

55) Narrated Abû Sa'îd Al-Khudri رضى الله عنه: I heard Prophet Muhammad صلى الله عليه وسلم saying: The devil said to his Lord: By Your Glory and Majesty! As long as the progeny of Adam

exists on earth, I shall continuously misguide them. At this Allâh remarked: By My Glory and Majesty! As long as they seek My forgiveness, I will go on to pardon them.

(This *Hadîth* is sound and reported by Ahmad in his *Musnad*).

To fight the Satan we should always perform the obligatory worshipping deeds timely e.g. Prayers, *Zakat*, Fasting etc. Besides, remembrance of Allah عز وجل is the best way out from the Satan traps.

****

(٥٦) عَنْ أَبِي هُرَيرَةَ رَضِيَ اللهُ عَنْهُ قَالَ: قَالَ رَسُوْلُ اللهِ ﷺ: «إِنَّ اللَّهَ إِذَا أَحَبَّ عَبْدًا دَعَا جِبْرِيْلَ فَقَالَ: إِنِّيْ أُحِبُّ فُلَانًا فَأَحِبَّهُ قَالَ: فَيُحِبُّهُ جِبْرِيْلُ ثُمَّ يُنَادِي فِي السَّمَاءِ فَيَقُوْلُ: إِنَّ اللَّهَ يُحِبُّ فُلَانًا فَأَحِبُّوهُ فَيُحِبُّهُ أَهْلُ السَّمَاءِ قَالَ ثُمَّ يُوْضَعُ لَهُ الْقَبُوْلُ فِي الأَرْضِ، وَإِذَا أَبْغَضَ عَبْدًا دَعَا جِبْرِيْلَ فَيَقُوْلُ: إِنِّي أَبْغَضُ فُلَانًا فَأَبْغِضْهُ قَالَ: فَيُبْغِضُهُ جِبْرِيْلُ ثُمَّ يُنَادِي فِي أَهْلِ السَّمَاءِ إِنَّ اللَّهَ يَبْغَضُ فُلَانًا فَأَبْغِضُوهُ قَالَ: فَيَبْغَضُوْنَهُ ثُمَّ تُوْضَعُ لَهُ الْبَغْضَاءُ فِي الأَرْضِ».

«حديث صحيح» [رواه مسلم والترمذي]

Sign of Allâh's love for His slave

56) Narrated Abû Huraira رضي الله عنه that Allâh's Messenger صلى الله عليه وسلم said: When Allâh loves a person, He calls Jibrael and says (to him): I love so-and-so, therefore you should also love him. The Prophet صلى الله عليه وسلم added: So, Jibrael begins to love him. Then he makes an announcement in the heaven saying: Allâh loves so-and-so, therefore you should also love him. Then the

inhabitants of heaven (the angels) would love him. He (صلى الله عليه وسلم) added: Thus acceptance is established for him on earth (i.e. that person becomes popular among the people). When Allâh dislikes any slave He calls Jibrael and says to him: I hate so-and-so, therefore you should also hate him. Then he calls out to the inhabitants of heaven: Allâh hates so-and-so, therefore you should also hate him. Thus hatred is established for him on earth (i.e., then hatred prevails against him among the people).

(This *Hadîth* is sound and reported by Muslim and Tirmidhi).

****

(٥٧) عَنْ أَبِي هُرَيرَةَ رَضِيَ اللهُ عَنْهُ قَالَ: قَالَ رَسُولُ اللهِ ﷺ: «إِنَّ اللَّهَ عَزَّ وَجلَّ يَقُولُ يَوْمَ الْقِيَامَةِ: يَا ابْنَ آدَمَ مَرِضْتُ فَلَمْ تَعُدْنِي قَالَ يَارَبِّ كَيْفَ أَعُودُكَ؟ وَأَنْتَ رَبُّ العَالَمِينَ. قَالَ أَمَا عَلِمْتَ أَنَّ عَبْدِي فُلاَنًا مَرِضَ فَلَمْ تَعُدْهُ، أَمَا عَلِمْتَ أَنَّكَ لَوْ عُدْتَهُ لَوَجَدْتَنِي عِنْدَهُ؟ يَا ابْنَ آدَمَ اسْتَطْعَمْتُكَ فَلَمْ تُطْعِمْنِي قَالَ: يَارَبِّ وَكَيْفَ أُطْعِمُكَ وَأَنْتَ رَبُّ العَالَمِينَ؟ قَالَ أَمَا عَلِمْتَ أَنَّهُ اسْتَطْعَمَكَ عَبْدِي فُلاَنٌ فَلَمْ تُطْعِمْهُ أَمَا عَلِمْتَ أَنَّكَ لَوْ أَطْعَمْتَهُ لَوَجَدْتَ ذَلِكَ عِنْدِي؟ يَاابْنَ آدَمَ اِسْتَسْقَيْتُكَ فَلَمْ تَسْقِنِي قَالَ: يَارَبِّ؟ كَيْفَ أَسْقِيكَ وَأَنْتَ رَبُّ العَالَمِينَ؟ قَالَ: اسْتَسْقَاكَ عَبْدِي فُلاَنٌ فَلَمْ تَسْقِهِ أَمَا إِنَّكَ لَوْ سَقَيْتَهُ وَجَدْتَ ذَلِكَ عِنْدِي». «حديث صحيح» [رواه مسلم]

Exhortation for developing mutual love and mercy among the Muslims

57) Narrated Abû Huraira رضى الله عنه that Allâh's Messenger صلى الله عليه وسلم said: Indeed Allâh عز وجل would say on the Day of Resurrection: O son of Adam! I fell ill but you visited Me not. He will say: How could I visit You while You are the Lord of the worlds? Allâh will say: Did you not know that My slave so-and-so was sick but you visited him not? Did you not know that if you had visited him, you would have found Me by him? O son of Adam! I asked you for food but you fed Me not. The slave will say: O Lord! How could I feed You whereas You are the Lord of the worlds? Allâh will say: Do you not know that such and such slave of Mine asked you for food but you did not feed him. Did you not know that if you had fed him, you would surely have found that with Me. O son of Adam! I asked you to give Me a drink but you gave Me not a drink. The slave will say: O Lord! How should I give You a drink while You are the Lord of the worlds? Allâh will say: My slave so-and-so asked you to give him a drink but you gave him no drink. Had you provided him a drink, you would have surely found the reward for doing so with Me.

(This *Hadîth* is sound and reported by Muslim).

As Allah عز وجل loves the believers, He commands them to love each other and feel the responsibility toward the poor, the starving, the naked etc. This is in addition to the compulsory *Zakat*, for more reward.

****

(٥٨) عَنْ أَبِي مَسْعُودٍ رَضِيَ اللهُ عَنْهُ قَالَ: قَالَ رَسُولُ اللهِ ﷺ: «حُوسِبَ رَجُلٌ مِمَّنْ كَانَ قَبْلَكُمْ فَلَمْ يُوجَدْ لَهُ مِنَ الْخَيْرِ

شَيْءٌ إِلاَّ أَنَّهُ كَانَ يُخَالِطُ النَّاسَ وَكَانَ مُوسِرًا فَكَانَ يَأْمُرُ غِلْمَانَهُ أَنْ يَتَجَاوَزُوْا عَنِ الْمُعْسِرِ قَالَ: قَالَ اللَّه عَزَّ وَجَلَّ: نَحْنُ أَحَقُّ بِذَلِكَ مِنْهُ تَجَاوَزُوا عَنْهُ». «حديث صحيح» [رواه مسلم]

Superiority of the one who granted a grave period to an insolvent

58) Narrated Abû Mas'ûd رضي الله عنه: Allâh's Messenger صلى الله عليه وسلم said: A man from among those who were before you was called to account by Allâh on the Day of Resurrection. No good was found in his account except that he used to mix with people and being a rich man, used to lend money to the people and order his servants to let off the men who are unable to repay debt. The Prophet صلى الله عليه وسلم said: Allâh عز وجل said to the angels: We are worthier than him of that generosity. So let him off.

(This *Hadîth* is sound and reported by Muslim).

Leave the one who is not in a position to repay his debt due to poor income.

****

(٥٩) عَنْ أَبِي هُرَيْرَةَ رَضِيَ اللهُ عَنْهُ أَنَّ رسول الله ﷺ قال: «إِنَّ رَجُلاً لَمْ يَعْمَلْ خَيْرًا قَطُّ وَكَانَ يُدَايِنُ النَّاسَ فَيَقُولُ لِرَسُولِهِ خُذْ مَا تَيَسَّرَ وَاتْرُكْ مَا عَسُرَ وَتَجَاوَزْ لَعَلَّ اللَّهَ تَعَالَى أَنْ يَتَجَاوَزَ عَنَّا فَلَمَّا هَلَكَ قَالَ اللَّهُ عَزَّ وَجَلَّ لَهُ: هَلْ عَمِلْتَ خَيْرًا قَطُّ؟ قَالَ: لاَ إِلاَّ أَنَّهُ كَانَ لِي غُلاَمٌ وَكُنْتُ أُدَايِنُ النَّاسَ فَإِذَا بَعَثْتُهُ لِيَتَقَاضَى قُلْتُ لَهُ: خُذْ مَاتَيَسَّرَ وَاتْرُكْ مَا عَسُرَ

وَتَجَاوَزْ لَعَلَّ اللَّهَ أَنْ يَتَجَاوَزَ عَنَّا قَالَ اللهُ تَعَالَى : قَدْ تَجَاوَزْتُ عَنْكَ» . «حديث حسن» [رواه النسائي]

59) Narrated Abû Huraira رضي الله عنه : Allâh's Messenger صلى الله عليه وسلم said: A man never did good deeds. Rather, he used to lend money to people and advise his servants: Take from the solvent and leave the insolvent and forgive him. Perhaps Allâh may forgive us. When he died, Allâh عز وجل asked him: Did you ever do anything good? He replied: No, but I had a servant and I used to lend people money. Whenever I sent him out to recover the loans, I advised him: Accept from the solvent and leave the one who is unable to repay. May Allâh forgive us, then Allâh the Exalted remarked: I have forgiven you.

(This *Hadîth* is good and reported by Nasa'i).

This wealthy man used to overlook his loans to the poor for the sake of Allah عز وجل, therefore, his reward was forgiveness in the Hereafter.

****

(٦٠) عنْ أَبِي هُرَيرَةَ رَضِيَ اللهُ عَنْهُ قَالَ : قَالَ رَسُولُ اللهِ ﷺ : «إِنَّ اللَّهَ يَقُولُ يَوْمَ الْقِيَامَةِ : أَيْنَ الْمُتَحَابُّونَ بِجَلاَلِي الْيَوْمَ أُظِلُّهُمْ فِي ظِلِّي يَوْمَ لاَ ظِلَّ إِلاَّ ظِلِّي» .

«حديث صحيح» [رواه مسلم]

Merit of love for the sake of Allâh

60) Narrated Abû Huraira رضي الله عنه: Allâh's Messenger صلى الله عليه وسلم said: Allâh will say on the Day of Resurrection: Where are those who love one another for My glory's sake. Today I will shelter them in My shade, today there is no shade but only My shade.

(This *Hadîth* is sound and reported by Muslim).

Equity, justice and social equity are the obligatory principles of Islam.

****

(٦١) عَنْ عُبَادَةَ بْنِ الصَّامِتِ رَضِيَ اللهُ عَنْهُ قَالَ: سَمِعْتُ رَسُولَ اللهِ ﷺ يَحْكِي عَنْ رَبِّهِ عَزَّ وَجَلَّ يَقُولُ: «حَقَّتْ مَحَبَّتِي لِلْمُتَحَابِّيْنَ فِيَّ وَحَقَّتْ مَحَبَّتِي لِلْمُتَبَاذِلِيْنَ فِيَّ وَحَقَّتْ مَحَبَّتِي لِلْمُتَزَاوِرِينَ فِيَّ، وَالمُتَحَابُّوْنَ فِي اللَّهِ عَلَى مَنَابِرِ مِنْ نُوْرٍ فِي ظِلِّ الْعَرْشِ يَوْمَ لاَ ظِلَّ إِلاَّ ظِلُّهُ». «حديث صحيح بمجموع طرقه» [رواه مسند أحمد]

61) Narrated 'Ubâda bin As-Sâmit رضي الله عنه: I heard Allâh's Messenger صلى الله عليه وسلم quoting his Lord عز وجل Who said: My love is established for those who love one another for My sake; and My love is established for those who spend money for My sake; and My love is established for those who visit one another for My sake. (In fact) those who love one another for the sake of Allâh will be at pulpits of light in the shade of Allah's Throne on a day when there is no shade but His shade.

(This *Hadîth* is sound through all its channels and reported in *Musnad Ahmad*).

****

(٦٢) عَنْ مُعَاذِ بْنِ جَبَلٍ رَضِيَ اللهُ عَنْهُ قَالَ: سَمِعْتُ رَسُولَ اللهِ ﷺ يَقُولُ: «قَالَ اللهُ عَزَّ وَجَلَّ: الْمُتَحَابُّونَ فِي جَلاَلِيْ لَهُمْ مَنَابِرُ مِنْ نُوْرٍ يَغْبِطُهُمُ النَّبِيُّوْنَ وَالشُّهَدَاءُ». «حديث حسن» [رواه الترمذي]

62) Narrated Mu'âdh bin Jabal رضى الله عنه: He said: I heard Allâh's Messenger صلى الله عليه وسلم saying: Allâh عز وجل said: For those who love one another for the sake of My glory there will be pulpits of light for which the Prophets and martyrs will envy them (on the Day of Resurrection).

(This *Hadîth* is good and reported by Tirmidhi).

****

(٦٣) عَنْ أَبِي هُرَيرَةَ رَضِيَ اللهُ عَنْهُ أَنَّ رَسُولَ اللهِ ﷺ قَالَ: «يَقُولُ اللهُ تَعَالَى: مَا لِعَبْدِي المُؤْمِنِ عِنْدِي جَزَاءٌ إِذَا قَبَضْتُ صَفِيَّهُ مِنْ أَهْلِ الدُّنْيَا ثُمَّ احْتَسَبَهُ إِلاَّ الجَنَّةَ».

«حديث صحيح» [رواه البخاري]

The merits of one who accepts the Will of Allâh at the death of one's son or a brother

63) Narrated Abû Huraira رضى الله عنه that Allâh's Messenger صلى الله عليه وسلم said: Allâh the Exalted says: I have nothing to give but Paradise as a reward to My believer-slave who, if I cause his son or brother to die, he bears it patiently for My reward.

(This *Hadîth* is sound and reported by Bukhâri).

****

(٦٤) عَنْ بَعْضِ أَصْحَابِ النَّبِيِّ ﷺ أَنَّهُ سَمِعَ النَّبِيَّ ﷺ يَقُولُ: «يُقَالُ لِلوِلْدَانِ يَوْمَ القِيَامَةِ ادْخُلُوا الجَنَّةَ، قَالَ: فَيَقُولُونَ يَارَبِّ حَتَّى يَدْخُلَ آبَاؤُنَاوَأُمَّهَاتُنَا، قَالَ: فَيَأْتُونَ قَالَ: فَيَقُولُ اللهُ عَزَّ وَجَلَّ مَالِي أَرَاهُمْ مُحْبَنْطِئِيْنَ ادْخُلُوا الْجَنَّةَ، قَالَ: فَيَقُولُونَ يَارَبِّ آبَاؤُنَا وَأُمَّهَاتُنَا، قَالَ: فَيَقُولُ ادْخُلُوا الجَنَّةَ أَنْتُمْ وَآبَاؤُكُمْ». «حديث صحيح» [رواه مسند أحمد]

64) Narrated some Companions of the Prophet صلى الله عليه وسلم that they heard the Prophet صلى الله عليه وسلم saying: On the Day of Resurrection, it would be said to the children: Get into Paradise. The Prophet صلى الله عليه وسلم said: They will say: O Lord! (We shall not enter Paradise) unless our fathers and mothers enter (with us). The Prophet صلى الله عليه وسلم added: They will be brought. Allâh عز وجل will say: What is the matter that they are reluctant to go to Paradise? The children will say: But what about our fathers and mothers! Allâh will say: Enter Paradise you and your parents.

(This *Hadîth* is sound and reported in *Musnad Ahmad*).

****

(٦٥) عَنْ أَبِي أُمَامَةَ رَضِيَ اللهُ عَنْهُ عَنِ النَّبِيِّ ﷺ قَالَ: «يَقُولُ اللهُ تَعَالَى: ابْنُ آدَمَ إِنْ صَبَرْتَ وَاحْتَسَبْتَ عِنْدَ الصَّدَمَةِ الأُوْلَى لَمْ أَرْضَ ثَوَابًا دُوْنَ الْجَنَّةِ».

«حديث حسن» [رواه ابن ماجه]

65) Narrated Abû Umama رضى الله عنه quoting the Prophet صلى الله عليه وسلم who said: Allâh سبحانه و تعالى says: Son of Adam! If you bear the first calamity (affliction) patiently for recompense, I shall not agree for you a reward less than Paradise.

****

(٦٦) عَنْ أَبِي مُوسَى الأَشْعَرِيِّ رَضِيَ اللهُ عَنْهُ قَالَ: قَالَ رَسُولُ اللهِ ﷺ: «إِذَا مَاتَ وَلَدُ العَبْدِ قَالَ اللهُ لِمَلاَئِكَتِهِ قَبَضْتُمْ وَلَدَ عَبْدِي فَيَقُولُونَ نَعَمْ فَيَقُولُ قَبَضْتُمْ ثَمْرَةَ فُؤَادِهِ فَيَقُولُونَ نَعَمْ فَيَقُوْلُ مَاذَا قَالَ عَبْدِي؟ فَيَقُولُونَ حَمِدَكَ وَاسْتَرْجَعَ فَيَقُولُ

اللهُ ابْنُوا لِعَبْدِي بَيْتًا فِي الجَنَّةِ وَسُمُّوهُ بَيْتَ الحَمْدِ» .

«حسنه الألباني» [رواه الترمذي وزوائد ابن حبان]

66) Narrated Abû Mûsa Al-Ashari رضي الله عنه: Allâh's Messenger صلى الله عليه وسلم said: When the son of a slave dies, Allâh says to His angels, though He knows best: You have taken away the soul of My slave's son. They say: Yes. Allâh says: You have taken out the fruit of his heart. They say: Yes. Then Allâh says: What did My slave say? They say: He praised You and read the words:

Allâh says (to the angels): Construct for My slave a house in Paradise (as a reward) and name it the 'The House of Praise'.

(Albani declared this *Hadîth* as good. It is reported by Tirmidhi and Ibn Hibban).

These *Ahadith* (plural of *Hadith*) highlight the superiority of patience over the loss of a beloved person (a son or brother). As we believe that the dead will be met in *Jannah* (Paradise) and that there is another eternal life, we should show Allah عز وجل our servitude and patience and hope to meet in *Jannah*, unlike the disbeliever who exaggerates at such a loss, because they are hopeless, and do not expect another life.

****

(٦٧) عَنْ عَبْدِ اللهِ بْنِ عُمْرِو بْنِ العَاصِ عَنْ رَسُولِ اللهِ ﷺ أَنَّهُ قَالَ: «هَلْ تَدْرُوْنَ أَوَّلَ مَنْ يَدْخُلُ الْجَنَّةَ مِنْ خَلْقِ اللهِ؟ قَالُوا: اَللهُ وَرَسُولُهُ أَعْلَمُ قَالَ: أَوَّلُ مَنْ يَدْخُلُ الجَنَّةَ مِنْ خَلْقِ اللهِ اَلْفُقَرَاءُ وَالْمُهَاجِرُوْنَ الَّذِيْنَ تُسَدُّ بِهِمُ الثُّغُوْرُ وَيُتَّقَى بِهِمُ الْمَكَارِهُ وَيَمُوْتُ أَحَدُهُمْ وَحَاجَتُهُ فِي صَدْرِهِ لاَ يَسْتَطِيعُ لَهَا

قَضَاءً فَيَقُوْلُ اللهُ عَزَّ وَجَلَّ لِمَنْ يَشَاءُ مِنْ مَلاَئِكَتِهِ: ائْتُوْهُمْ فَحَيُّوْهُمْ فَتَقُوْلُ الْمَلاَئِكَةُ: نَحْنُ سُكَّانُ سَمَائِكَ وَخِيرَتُكَ مِنْ خَلْقِكَ أَفَتَأْمُرُنَا أَنْ نَأْتِي هَؤُلاَءِ فَنُسَلِّمَ عَلَيْهِمْ؟!! قَالَ: إِنَّهُمْ كَانُوْا عِبَادًا يَعْبُدُوْنِي لاَيُشْرِكُونَ بِي شَيْئًا وَتُسَدُّ بِهِمُ الثُّغُوْرُ وَيُتَّقَى بِهِمُ المَكَارِهُ وَيَمُوْتُ أَحَدُهُمْ وَحَاجَتُهُ فِي صَدْرِهِ لاَيَسْتَطِيْعُ لَهَا قَضَاءً قَالَ فَتَأْتِيهُمُ المَلاَئِكَةُ عِنْدَ ذَلِكَ فَيَدْخُلُونَ عَلَيْهِمْ مِنْ كُلِّ بَابٍ ﴿سَلاَمٌ عَلَيْكُمْ بِمَا صَبَرْتُمْ فَنِعْمَ عُقْبَى الدَّارِ﴾». «حديث صحيح لغيره» [رواه مسند أحمد]

67) Narrated 'Abdullâh bin Amr bin Al-Aas that Allâh's Messenger صلى الله عليه وسلم said: Do you know the first of Allâh's creation to enter Paradise? They said: Allâh and His Messenger صلى الله عليه وسلم know best. He said: The first of Allâh's creation to enter Paradise will be the poor and the emigrants through whom the boundaries are guarded and calamities are prevented. Their condition is that when anyone of them dies, his wish remains in his chest unfulfilled. Allâh عزوجل says to whom He likes from among the angels: Go to them and greet them. The angels say: We are inhabitants of Your heaven and are the choicest of Your creation and still You want us to go and offer greetings to them? Allâh says: Indeed they are the slaves who worship Me alone and associate none with Me (in any form of worship). Through them the boundaries are guarded and calamities are prevented. When anyone of them is dead, his wish remains in his chest unfulfilled. He said: So the angels will come to them and enter upon them

from each door saying:

"*Salâmun 'Alaikum* (peace be upon you) for that you persevered in patience! Excellent indeed is the final home (of yours)!

This *Hadîth* is considered sound by others, and reported in *Musnad Ahmad*).

Poverty is sometimes a virtue. You live simple, and your reckoning will be simple and easy. More wealth means that you have to justify how you gained it and where you spent it.

****

(٦٨) عَنْ أَبِي هُرَيْرَةَ رَضِيَ اللهُ عَنْهُ أَنَّ رَسُولَ اللهِ ﷺ قَالَ:

«قَالَ اللهُ: أَنْفِقْ يَاابْنَ آدَمَ أُنْفِقْ عَلَيْكَ»

«حديث صحيح» [رواه البخاري ومسلم]

Superiority of spending on good works and enjoining that

68) Narrated Abû Huraira رضى الله عنه that Allâh's Messenger صلى الله عليه وسلم said: Spend, O son of Adam! and I shall spend on you.

(This *Hadîth* is sound and reported by Bukhâri and Muslim).

This *Hadith* signifies that a faithful believer should spend money in Allah's cause as ordained by Him. Consequently Allah will spend on him and bestow him with His favours in the world.

****

(٦٩) عَنْ عَدِي بْنِ حَاتِمٍ رَضِيَ اللهُ عَنْهُ قَالَ: كُنْتُ عِنْدَ

رَسُولِ اللهِ ﷺ فَجَاءَهُ رَجُلَانِ أَحَدُهُمَا يَشْكُو الْعِيْلَةَ وَالآخَرُ

يَشْكُو قَطْعَ السَّبِيْلِ فَقَالَ رَسُولُ اللهِ ﷺ: «أَمَّا قَطْعُ السَّبِيْلِ فَإِنَّهُ

لاَيَأْتِي عَلَيْكَ إِلاَّ قَلِيْلٌ حَتَّى تَخْرُجَ العِيْرُ مِنْ مَكَّةَ بِغَيْرِ خَفِيْرٍ ، وَأَمَّا العِيْلَةُ فَإِنَّ السَّاعَةَ لاَ تَقُوْمُ حَتَّى يَطُوْفَ أَحَدُكُمْ بِصَدَقَتِهِ لاَ يَجِدُ مَنْ يَقْبَلُهَا مِنْهُ ثُمَّ لَيَقِفَنَّ أَحَدُكُمْ بَيْنَ يَدي اللهِ لَيْسَ بَيْنَهُ وَبَيْنَهُ حِجَابٌ وَلاَ تَرْجُمَانٌ يُتَرْجِمُ ثُمَّ لَيَقُوْلَنَّ لَهُ: أَلَمْ أُوْتِكَ مَالاً؟ فَلَيَقُوْلَنَّ: بَلَى ثُمَّ لَيَقُوْلَنَّ: أَلَمْ أُرْسِلْ إِلَيْكَ رَسُولاً؟ فَلَيَقُوْلَنَّ: بَلَى فَيَنْظُرُ عَنْ يَمِيْنِهِ فَلاَ يَرَى إِلاَّ النَّارَ ثُمَّ يَنْظُرُ عَنْ شِمَالِهِ فَلاَ يَرَى إِلاَّ النَّارَ فَلْيَتَّقِيَنَّ أَحَدُكُمُ النَّارَ وَلَوْ بِشِقِّ تَمْرَةٍ فَإِنْ لَمْ يَجِدْ فَبِكَلِمَةٍ طَيِّبَةٍ».

«حديث صحيح» . [رواه البخاري]

69) Narrated 'Adi bin Hâtim رضى الله عنه: I was (sitting) with Allâh's Messenger صلى الله عليه وسلم. There came to him two men. One of them was complaining of poverty while the other was complaining against brigandage. Allâh's Messenger صلى الله عليه وسلم said: As for brigandage, it will be a short time before a caravan sets out from Makkah (on a journey) without security guards. As regards poverty, the Hour will not be established until anyone of you goes around with his charity but fails to find any due recipients of it. Then one of you will stand before Allâh. There will be no screen between Allah and him, nor will be there an interpreter to translate for him. Allâh will ask him: Did I not grant you wealth? He will say: Yes. Then he will look at his right side and will see nothing except Fire. Then he will look to his left side and will see nothing but Fire. The Prophet added: So let each of you protect himself against Hell even if with half a date, or, if not available, with a kind word.

(This *Hadîth* is sound and reported by Bukhâri).

The precept of this *Hadith* is that soon there will be so good peace and law and order to the extent that a caravan from Makkah on a journey to San'â (Yemen) will not need escorts against robbers. Further, the people will prosper economically to the extent that nobody will accept charity. This *Hadith* also implies that on the Day of Resurrection where there will be nothing to intervene between Allah and His slave, a believer will be asked about his beliefs, deeds and wealth. So a believer should act in pursuance of Islam and protect himself against Fire by either half a date or a kind word to please people.

****

(٧٠) عَنْ أَبِي وَاقِدٍ اللَّيْثِي رَضِيَ اللهُ عَنْهُ قَالَ: كُنَّا نَأْتِي النَّبِيَّ ﷺ إِذَا أُنْزِلَ عَلَيْهِ فَيُحَدِّثُنَا فَقَالَ لَنَا ذَاتَ يَوْمٍ: «إِنَّ اللهَ عَزَّ وَجَلَّ قَالَ: إِنَّا أَنْزَلْنَا المَالَ لإِقَامِ الصَّلاَةِ وَإِيْتَاءِ الزَّكَاةِ وَلَوْ كَانَ لابْنِ آدَمَ وَادٍ لأَحَبَّ أَنْ يَكُوْنَ إِلَيهِ ثَانٍ وَلَوْ كَانَ لَهُ وَادِيَانِ لأَحَبَّ أَنْ يَكُوْنَ إِلَيْهِمَا ثَالِثٌ وَلاَ يَمْلأُ جَوْفَ ابْنِ آدَمَ إِلاَّ التُّرَابُ ثُمَّ يَتُوْبُ اللهُ عَلَى مَنْ تَابَ» . «حديث حسن» [رواه مسند أحمد]

Nothing but sand can satisfy fully the belly of Son of Adam

70) Narrated Abû Wâqid Al-Laithi رضي الله عنه: We used to visit the Prophet صلى الله عليه وسلم to hear anything revealed to him. One day he said to us: Allâh عزوجل said: Verily, We have bestowed (the believers) with fortune in order to offer prayers and pay *Zakât* (as per rules). But if the son of Adam had one valley of money he would wish for the second. If he had two valleys, he would wish for the third, So, nothing except soil can fill up the belly of the son of

Adam. But Allâh will forgive the one who repents to Him.

(This *Hadîth* is good and reported in *Musnad Ahmad*).

****

(٧١) عَنْ عُقْبَةَ بْنِ عَامِرٍ رَضِيَ اللهُ عَنْهُ قَالَ: سَمِعْتُ رَسُولَ اللهِ ﷺ يَقُولُ: «يَقُومُ الرَّجُلُ مِنْ أُمَّتِي مِنَ اللَّيْلِ يُعَالِجُ نَفْسَهُ إِلَى الطَّهُورِ وَعَلَيْهِ عُقَدٌ فَإِذَا وَضَّأَ يَدَيْهِ انْحَلَّتْ عُقْدَةٌ وَإِذَا وَضَّأَ وَجْهَهُ انْحَلَّتْ عُقْدَةٌ وَإِذَا مَسَحَ رَأْسَهُ انْحَلَّتْ عُقْدَةٌ وَإِذَا وَضَّأَ رِجْلَيْهِ انْحَلَّتْ عُقْدَةٌ فَيَقُولُ اللهُ عَزَّ وَجَلَّ لِلَّذِيْنَ وَرَاءَ الْحِجَابِ انْظُرُوا إِلَى عَبْدِي هَذَا يُعَالِجُ نَفْسَهُ يَسْأَلُنِي مَا سَأَلَنِي عَبْدِى هَذَا فَهُوَ لَهُ». «حديث صحيح» [رواه أحمد وزوائد ابن حبان]

Superiority of making ablution at night (i.e. praying)

71) Narrated Uqba bin Aamir رضى الله عنه: I heard Allâh's Messenger صلى الله عليه وسلم saying: One of my followers gets up at night pushing himself to perform ablution (for prayer). On him there are several knots of the Satan. When he washes his hands, a knot loosens. When he washes his face, another knot loosens. When he passes his wet hands over his head, yet another knot loosens. When he washes his legs, the last knot loosens. Then Allâh عزوجل says to those beyond the eyes (angels): Look at this slave of Mine who cures his inner-self and asks Me forgiveness. So, what he asks is given to him.

(This *Hadîth* is sound and reported by Ibn Hibban and Ahmad in his *Musnad*).

This *Hadith* shows that wealth is given to a Muslim so that he may perform prayers perfectly and pay the annual charges known as *Zakat* in Islam. But the human being is so greedy that he knows no extent to his desires. He goes on collecting wealth until the last breath.

****

(٧٢) عَنْ أَبِي هُرَيرَةَ رَضِيَ اللهُ عَنْهُ أَنَّ رَسُولَ اللهِ ﷺ قَالَ:

«يَنْزِلُ رَبُّنَا تَبَارَكَ وَتَعَالَى كُلَّ لَيْلَةٍ إِلَى السَّمَاءِ الدُّنْيَا حِيْنَ يَبْقَى ثُلُثُ اللَّيْلِ الآخِرِ يَقُولُ: مَنْ يَدْعُونِي فَأَسْتَجِيْبَ لَهُ مَنْ يَسْأَلُنِي فَأُعْطِيَهُ مَنْ يَسْتَغْفِرُنِي فَأَغْفِرَ لَهُ».

« حديث صحيح » [رواه البخاري ومسلم وأصحاب السنن]

Superiority of supplication at night

72) Narrated Abû Huraira رضى الله عنه that Allâh's Messenger صلى الله عليه وسلم said: In the last third of every night our Lord تبارك وتعالى descends to the lowermost heaven and says: Who is calling Me, so that I may answer him? Who is asking Me, so that I may grant him? Who is seeking forgiveness from Me, so that I may forgive him.

(This *Hadîth* is sound and reported in *Musnad* of Abû Ya'la).

Late at night when people get much busy with worldly pleasures, Allah عز وجل gives the believers an opportunity, or say, an answer hour if they can fight sleep and invoke Allah for whatever they need. In another *Hadith* in this book, Allah عز وجل is said to descend to the lowest heaven saying: Who asks My forgivenss so that I forgive him, and who wants something so that I grant it to him.

****

(٧٣) عَنِ ابْنِ مَسْعُودٍ رَضِيَ اللهُ عَنْهُ عَنِ النَّبِيِّ ﷺ قَالَ: «عَجِبَ رَبُّنَا عَزَّ وَجَلَّ مِنْ رَجُلَيْنِ: رَجُلٍ ثَارَ عَنْ وِطَائِهِ وَلِحَافِهِ مِنْ بَيْنِ أَهْلِهِ وَحَيِّهِ إِلَى صَلاَتِهِ فَيَقُوْلُ رَبُّنَا: أَيَا مَلاَئِكَتِي انْظُرُوا إِلَى عَبْدِي ثَارَ مِنْ فِرَاشِهِ وَوِطَائِهِ وَمِنْ بَيْنِ حَيِّهِ وَأَهْلِهِ إِلَى صَلاَتِهِ رَغْبَةً فِيْمَا عِنْدِي وَشَفَقَةً مِمَّا عِنْدِي. وَرَجُلٍ غَزَا فِي سَبِيْلِ اللهِ فَانْهَزَمُوْا فَعَلِمَ مَا عَلَيْهِ مِنَ الْفِرَارِ وَمَالَهُ فِي الرُّجُوْعِ فَرَجَعَ حَتَّى أُهْرِيْقَ دَمُهُ رَغْبَةً فِيْمَا عِنْدِي وَشَفَقَةً مِمَّا عِنْدِي فَيَقُوْلُ اللهُ عَزَّ وَجَلَّ لِمَلاَئِكَتِهِ انْظُرُوا إِلَى عَبْدِي رَجَعَ رَغْبَةً فِيْمَا عِنْدِي وَرَهْبَةً مِمَّا عِنْدِي حَتَّى أُهْرِيْقَ دَمُهُ». «حديث حسن»

[مسند أحمد وأبو داؤود وزوائد ابن حبان والحاكم في المستدرك]

Our Lord عزوجل wonders at two men

73) Narrated Ibn Mas'ûd رضى الله عنه : The Prophet صلى الله عليه وسلم said: Our Lord عزوجل wonders at two men: One is he who got out of his bed and quitted from among his family and tribesmen to perform prayers. Our Lord says: O My angels! Look at this slave of Mine who got up from his bed and quitted from among his tribesmen to offer prayers desiring what is available with Me and fearing what is with Me. Second is he who fought in Allâh's cause and got defeated along with his fellow fighters. But he knew what punishment he will suffer in case of fleeing from the battlefield and what reward he will get in returning to the battlefield. So he returned (and fought against Allâh's enemies) until he was killed desiring what is with Me and

awing from what is with Me. Allâh عزوجل says to his angels (wonderingly): Look at My slave who returned (to the battlefield) hoping for what is with Me and fearing what is with Me until his blood was shed.

(This *Hadîth* is good and reported by Ahmad, Abû Dâ'ud, Ibn Hibban and Al-Hakim).

Allah's عـزوجـل wonder is meant for His admiration and appreciation of the fighters' premeditation and patience to die for the sake of Allah. Getting up at night and praying is not also an easy thing; only real devotees can do that, let alone those who leave the Dawn prayers and sleep.

****

(٧٤) عَنْ أَبِي هُرَيْرَةَ رَضِيَ اللهُ عَنْهُ أَنَّ رَسُولَ اللهِ ﷺ قَالَ:
«أَوَّلُ مَا يُحَاسَبُ بِهِ الْعَبْدُ صَلاَتُهُ فَإِنْ كَانَ أَكْمَلَهَا وَإِلاَّ قَالَ اللهُ
عَزَّ وَجَلَّ انْظُرُوا لِعَبْدِي مِنْ تَطَوُّعٍ فَإِنْ وُجِدَ لَهُ تَطَوُّعٌ قَالَ
أَكْمِلُوا بِهِ الْفَرِيضَةَ». «حديث صحيح» [رواه النسائي]

Superiority of Voluntary prayers

74) Narrated Abû Huraira رضى الله عنه that Allâh's Messenger صلى الله عليه وسلم said: First of the deeds for which a slave will be called to account (on the Day of Resurrection) will be his (obligatory) prayers. If they are complete (he has prospered and succeeded), otherwise Allâh عزوجل will say (to the angels): See whether there are any (voluntary) prayers of My slave. If any, Allâh will say: Complete his obligatory prayers with them.

(This *Hadîth* is sound and reported by Ahmad in his *Musnad*, Abû Dâ'ud and Ibn Hibban).

On the Day of Resurrection, a believer will be first held accountable for his obligatory prayers. If they are in order, he has succeeded. If they are wanting, the angels will be commanded to check his voluntary prayers, if any, they will make for the loss in his obligatory prayers. Then the rest of his acts will be judged.

****

(٧٥) عُنْ عُقْبَةَ بْنِ عَامِرٍ رَضِيَ اللهُ عَنْهُ قَالَ : سَمِعْتُ رَسُولَ اللهِ ﷺ يَقُولُ : «يَعْجَبُ رَبُّكُمْ مِنْ رَاعِي غَنَمٍ فِي رَأْسِ شَظِيَّةٍ بِجَبَلٍ يُؤَذِّنُ بِالصَّلَاةِ وَيُصَلِّي فَيَقُولُ اللهُ عَزَّ وَجَلَّ انْظُرُوْا إِلَى عَبْدِي هَذَا يُؤَذِّنُ وَيُقِيْمُ الصَّلَاةَ يَخَافُ مِنِّي قَدْ غَفَرْتُ لِعَبْدِى وَأَدْخَلْتُهُ الْجَنَّةَ» . «حديث صحيح»

[رواه أبو داؤد والنسائي وزائد ابن حبان]

Merits of raising the (*Adhân*) prayer-call

75) Narrated Uqba bin Aamir رضى الله عنه: I heard Allâh's Messenger صلى الله عليه وسلم saying: Your Lord wonders at a shepherd who on the peak of a mountain pronounces *Adhân* for prayers and offers them. Then Allâh عزوجل says (to the angels): Look at this slave of Mine who calls for prayer and performs it all by himself. He fears Me. So I have forgiven My slave and admitted him to Paradise.

(This *Hadîth* is sound and reported by Abû Dâ'ud, Nasa'i and Ibn Hibban).

This *Hadith* shows that calling for prayer and praying all by yourself is recommended, if you travel alone or say be assigned to a job alone.

****

(٧٦) عَنْ أَبي هُرَيرَةَ رَضِيَ اللهُ عَنْهُ أَنَّ رَسُولَ اللهِ ﷺ قَالَ: «يَتَعَاقَبُونَ فِيكُمْ مَلاَئِكَةٌ بِاللَّيْلِ وَمَلاَئِكَةٌ بِالنَّهَارِ وَيَجْتَمِعُونَ فِي صَلاَةِ الفَجْرِ وَصَلاَةِ العَصْرِ ثُمَّ يَعْرُجُ الَّذِينَ بَاتُوا فِيكُمْ فَيَسْأَلُهُمْ - وَهُوَ أَعْلَمُ بِهِمْ - كَيْفَ تَرَكْتُمْ عِبَادِي فَيَقُولُونَ: تَرَكْنَاهُمْ وَهُمْ يُصَلُّونَ وَأَتَيْنَاهُمْ وَهُمْ يُصَلُّونَ». «حديث صحيح»

[رواه البخاري ومسلم]

Superiority of *Fajr* and *Asr* Prayers

76) Narrated Abû Huraira رضى الله عنه that Allâh's Messenger صلى الله عليه وسلم said: Some angels come to you in succession by night and some others come to you by day. they meet together at the time of Dawn (*Fajr*) and Afternoon (*Asr*) prayers. Then those who passed the night with you, ascend to heaven. There Allâh asks them though He knows best about them: In what state did you leave My slaves? The angels reply: When we left them, they were offering prayers and when we reached them, they were offering prayers.

(This *Hadîth* is sound and reported by Bukhâri and Muslim).

The most important prayers are the Dawn (*Fajr*) and Afternoon (*Asr*) ones. Perhaps because one has to fight tendency for sleep and rest at these times. *Asr* prayer is mostly the mid-prayer Allah عز وجل asserted in the Qur'ân:

"Guard strictly the (five) prayers especially, the mid-prayer (*Asr*).." (2:238)

****

(٧٧) عَنْ عَبْدِ اللهِ بْنِ عَمْرٍو رَضِيَ اللهُ عَنْهُمَا قَالَ: صَلَّيْنَا مَعَ رَسُوْلِ اللهِ ﷺ المَغْرِبَ فَرَجَعَ مَنْ رَجَعَ وَعَقَّبَ مَنْ عَقَّبَ فَجَاءَ رَسُوْلُ اللهِ ﷺ مُسْرِعًا قَدْ حَفَزَهُ النَّفَسُ وَقَدْ حَسَرَ عَنْ رُكْبَتَيْهِ فَقَالَ: «أَبْشِرُوْا هَذَا رَبُّكُمْ قَدْ فَتَحَ بَابًا مِنْ أَبْوَابِ السَّمَاءِ يُبَاهِي بِكُمُ الْمَلاَئِكَةَ يَقُوْلُ: انْظُرُوْا إِلَى عِبَادِي قَدْ قَضَوْا فَرِيْضَةً وَهُمْ يَنْتَظِرُوْنَ أُخْرَى». «حديث صحيح»

[رواه ابن ماجه وأحمد]

Superiority of staying in the mosque from *Maghrib* (Evening) prayer to *'Ishâ'* (Night) prayer

77) Narrated 'Abdullâh bin Amr رضى الله عنهما: Once we performed *Maghrib* (Evening) prayer along with Allâh's Messenger صلى الله عليه وسلم, then some people left while some others stayed behind in the mosque. Shortly afterwards, Allâh's Messenger صلى الله عليه وسلم came fast in a state that he was panting violently and his knees were uncovered. He said excitedly: Be happy. This is your Lord who has opened a gate of the heavens. He talked to the angels proudly about you and said: Look at these slaves of Mine. They have just finished one obligatory prayer and are now waiting for the next.

(This *Hadîth* is sound and reported by Ibn Mâjah and Ahmad in his *Musnad*).

Waiting for a prayer, having performed the first is a great deed, the reward of which is greater ten times or more, if you wait voluntarily for that.

****

(٧٨) عَنْ نَعِيْمِ بْنِ هَمَّارٍ الغَطْفَانِي أَنَّهُ سَمِعَ رَسُولَ اللهِ ﷺ يقُولُ : «قَالَ اللهُ عَزَّ وَجَلَّ : يَاابْنَ آدَمَ لاَ تَعْجَزْ عَنْ أَرْبَعِ رَكَعَاتٍ مِنْ أَوَّلِ النَّهَارِ أَكْفِكَ آخِرَهُ» . «حديث صحيح»

[رواه أحمد وأبوداؤود وزوائد ابن حبان]

Superiority of performance of four *Rak'at* at the forenoon

78) Narrated Na'im bin Hammar Al-Ghatfani that he heard Allâh's Messenger صلى الله عليه وسلم saying: Allâh عزوجل said: O son of Adam! Don't feel short of performing four *Ruk'at* (prayer) at the forenoon. (If you do so) I will safeguard you (against the Satan) for the rest of the day.

(This *Hadîth* is sound and reported by Ahmad in his *Musnad* and Abû Dâ'ud and Ibn Hibban).

Voluntary prayers are mostly preferable at the night, but the Prophet صلى الله عليه وسلم used to perform two (*Raka'*) by day in the forenoon. This is known to be the *Duha* prayer. It can also be four *Raka'* or more; six or eight if you like.

****

(٧٩) عَنْ أَبِي هُرَيرَةَ رَضِيَ اللهُ عَنْهُ أَنَّ رَسُولَ اللهِ ﷺ قَالَ : «أَلاَ أُعَلِّمُكَ ـ أَوْ قَالَ أَلاَ أَدُلُّكَ عَلَى ـ كَلِمَةٍ مِنْ تَحْتِ العَرْشِ مِنْ كَنْزِ الجَنَّةِ؟! تَقُولُ : لاَ حَوْلَ وَلاَ قُوَّةَ إِلاَّ بِاللهِ فَيَقُولُ اللهُ عَزَّ وَجَلَّ : أَسْلَمَ عَبْدِي وَاسْتَسْلَمَ» . «حديث حسن»

[رواه مستدرك الحاكم]

Superiority of *La haula wa la quwwata illa Billah* (There is no power and might except by Allâh)

79) Narrated Abû Huraira رضى الله عنه that Allâh's Messenger said: Should I not teach you or (probably) said: Shall I not show you a word from under the Divine Throne of Allah out of the treasure of Paradise? You should say لاحول ولاقوة الابالله (There is no power and no strength except by Allâh). At this Allâh عزوجل will say: My slave has become a Muslim and has surrendered himself to My Will.

(This *Hadîth* is good and reported in *Mustadrak* of Al-Hâkim).

This phrase لاحول ولا قوة الا بالله (No power or might except Allah's) is one of the highly rewarded as لا اله الا الله (There is no God, but Allah) and الله اكبر (Allah is All-Great).

****

(٨٠) عَنْ أَبِي هُرَيْرَةَ رَضِيَ اللهُ قَالَ قَالَ رَسُوْلُ اللهِ ﷺ:

«إِنَّ اللهَ عَزَّ وَجَلَّ لَيَرْفَعُ الدَّرَجَةَ لِلْعَبْدِ الصَّالِحِ فِي الْجَنَّةِ فَيَقُوْلُ: يَارَبِّ أَنَّى لِي هَذِهِ فَيَقُوْلُ: بِاسْتِغْفَارِ وَلَدِكَ لَكَ».

«حديث حسن» [رواه أحمد]

Superiority of asking forgiveness by a son for his parents

80) Narrated Abû Huraira رضى الله عنه: Allâh's Messenger صلى الله عليه وسلم said: Allâh عزوجل will raise the rank of a righteous

slave in Paradise and the slave will say: O Lord! From where has this come to me? Allâh will say: Yes. This is because of your son who has been asking forgiveness for you.

(This *Hadîth* is good and reported in *Musnad* of Ahmad).

If your parents die as Muslims you can invoke Allah for them, even perform *Hajj* and spend money on the poor on their behalf. *But* be careful and do not do that, if they were not Muslims.

****

(٨١) عَنِ ابْنِ عَبَّاسٍ رَضِيَ اللهُ عَنْهُمَا قَالَ: قَالَ رَسُولُ اللهِ ﷺ: «قَالَ إِبْلِيسُ: يَارَبِّ لَيْسَ أَحَدٌ مِنْ خَلْقِكَ إِلاَّ جَعَلْتَ لَهُ رِزْقًا وَمَعِيشَةً فَمَا رِزْقِي؟ قَالَ: مَالَمْ يُذْكَرِ اسْمُ اللهِ عَلَيْهِ».

«حديث صحيح» [رواه أبو نعيم في الحلية]

Satan's provision (sustenance)

81) Narrated Ibn 'Abbâs رضي الله عنهما: Allâh's Messenger صلى الله عليه وسلم said: *Iblis* (Fiend) said: O Lord! For every one of Your creatures You have arranged sustenance and means of livelihood but what is mine? Allâh said: Anything on which Allâh's Name is not mentioned (can be yours).

(This *Hadîth* is reported by Abû Na'im in his book *Al-Hilya* and its chain of authorities is sound).

You have according to this Prophetic tradition; to mention the Name of Allah عز وجل and say (In the Name of Allah) before you take any food or a drink or even do anything, to stop *Iblis* (fiend) as well as all other satans.

****

(٨٢) عَنْ عُبَادَةَ بْنِ الصَّامِتِ رَضِيَ اللهُ عَنْهُ قَالَ: سَمِعْتُ رَسُولَ اللهِ ﷺ يَقُولُ: «إِنَّ أَوَّلَ مَا خَلَقَ اللهُ الْقَلَمُ فقَالَ لَهُ: اكْتُبْ قَالَ: رَبِّ وَمَاذَا أَكْتُبُ؟ قَالَ: اكْتُبْ مَقَادِيْرَ كُلِّ شَيْءٍ حَتَّى تَقُوْمَ السَّاعَةُ». «حديث صحيح لغيره» [أحمد وأبو داؤود]

The first creation of Allâh

82) Narrated 'Ubâda bin As-Sâmit رضى الله عنه: I heard Allâh's Messenger صلى الله عليه وسلم saying: The first thing created by Allâh was the pen. He said to it: Write. It said: O Lord! What should I write? Allâh said: Write down the destiny of every thing until the Final Hour (as per My Will).

(This *Hadîth* is sound and reported in *Musnad* of Ahmad).

****

(٨٣) عَنْ عَبْدِ الرَّحْمٰنِ بْنِ عَوْفٍ رَضِيَ اللهُ عَنْهُ قَالَ: قَالَ رَسُولُ اللهِ ﷺ: «إِنَّ جِبْرِيلَ عَلَيْهِ السَّلاَمُ قَالَ لِي: أَلاَ أُبَشِّرُكَ إِنَّ اللهَ عَزَّ وَجَلَّ يَقُوْلُ لَكَ مَنْ صَلَّى عَلَيْكَ صَلَّيْتُ عَلَيْهِ وَمَنْ سَلَّمَ عَلَيْكَ سَلَّمْتُ عَلَيْهِ». «حديث حسن لغيره»

[رواه أحمد والبيهقي في سننه الكبرى وأبو يعلى]

Superiority of saying: peace be upon the Prophet

83) Narrated Abdur-Rahmân bin Auf رضى الله عنه: Allâh's Messenger صلى الله عليه وسلم said: Once Jibrael (Gabriel) said to

me: Should I tell you something good Allâh عزوجل says to you: Who ever prays for you by saying صلى الله عليه و سلم, I will give him My blessing and mercy and who sends to you greetings, I will sent to him My greetings.

(This *Hadîth* is considered good by others, and reported by Ahmad in his *Musnad*, Al-Baihaqi and Abû Ya'la).

The remembrance and repetition of صلى الله عليه وسلم (peace and blessing of Allah be upon Muhammad) is highly rewarded and it is one of the causes of the Prophet صلى الله عليه وسلم intercession in the Hereafter. The more you say that the better you deserve the intercession.

****

(٨٤) عَنْ أَبِي سَعِيْدٍ الْخُدْرِيِّ رَضِيَ اللهُ عَنْهُ قَالَ: سَمِعْتُ رَسُولَ اللهِ ﷺ يَقُولُ: «إِنَّ اللهَ لَيَسْأَلُ الْعَبْدَ يَوْمَ الْقِيَامَةِ حَتَّى يَقُوْلَ: مَا مَنَعَكَ إِذْ رَأَيْتَ الْمُنْكَرَ أَنْ تُنْكِرَهُ؟ فَإِذَا لَقَّنَ اللهُ عَبْدًا حُجَّتَهُ قَالَ: يَارَبِّ رَجَوْتُكَ وَفَرَقْتُ مِنَ النَّاسِ».

«حديث حسن» [رواه ابن ماجه وزوائد ابن حبان]

Inducement of good and Prohibition of evil

84) Narrated Abû Sa'îd Al-Khudri رضى الله عنه: I heard Allâh's Messenger صلى الله عليه وسلم saying: Allâh will question His slave on the Day of Resurrection and say: What prevented you, when you saw an objectionable act, from prohibiting it? So when Allâh inspires the slave he would say: O Lord! I hoped for Your forgiveness and feared the people.

(This *Hadîth* is good and reported by Ibn Mâjah and Ibn Hibban).

Ibn Qaiyim Al-Jawzi mentioned in his books many types of *Jihad* (fighting in the way of Allah عز وجل), one type is: commanding good deeds and preventing vice. It is also a sign of piety, e.g. wherever there is this activity the community is healthy. If there is no commanding of good and prevention of vice, this means that Islam is not well applied or followed.

****

(٨٥) عَنْ أَبِي هُرَيرَةَ رَضِيَ اللهُ عَنْهُ قَالَ: سَمِعْتُ رَسُولَ اللهِ ﷺ يَقُولُ: «قَالَ اللهُ تَعَالَى قَسَمْتُ الصَّلاَةَ بَيْنِى وَبَيْنَ عَبْدِي نِصْفَيْنِ وَلِعَبْدِي مَا سَأَلَ فَإِذَا قَالَ الْعَبْدُ: الْحَمْدُ للهِ رَبِّ الْعَالَمِيْنَ قَالَ اللهَ تَعَالَى: حَمَدَنِي عَبْدِي، وَإِذَا قَالَ: الرَّحْمٰنِ الرَّحِيْمِ قَالَ اللهُ تَعَالَى: أَثْنى عَلَيَّ عَبْدِي وَإِذَا قَالَ: مَالِكِ يَوْمِ الدِّيْنِ قَالَ: مَجَّدَنِي عَبْدِي ﴿وَقَالَ مَرَّةً: فَوَّضَ إِلَيَّ عَبْدِي﴾ فَإِذَا قَالَ: إِيَّاكَ نَعْبُدُ وَإِيَّاكَ نَسْتَعِيْنَ قَالَ: هَذَا بَيْنِيْ وَبَيْنَ عَبْدِي وَلِعَبْدِي مَا سَأَلَ فَإِذَا قَالَ: اهْدِنَا الصِّرَاطَ الْمُسْتَقِيْمَ، صِرَاطَ الَّذِيْنَ أَنْعَمْتَ عَلَيْهِمْ غَيْرِ الْمَغْضُوبِ عَلَيْهِمْ وَلاَ الضَّالِّيْنَ قَالَ: هَذَا لِعَبْدِي وَلِعَبْدِي مَا سَأَلَ». «حديث صحيح»

[رواه مسلم وأصحاب السنن]

Superiority of *Surat Al-Fâtiha* (the Opening *Surah*)

85) Narrated Abû Huraira رضى الله عنه: I heard Allâh's

Messenger صلى الله عليه وسلم saying that Allâh said: I have divided the prayer into two halves between Me and My slave. My slave will have what he asks for. When the slave recites: All praises be to Allâh, the Lord of the worlds, Allâh says: My slave has praised Me. When the slave recites: The Most Gracious, the Most Merciful, Allâh says: My slave has modifid Me best. When the slave recites: He is the Owner of the Day of Judgment. Allâh says: My slave has glorified Me and once He says: My slave has surrendered himself to My Will. When the slave recites: You we worship and from You we seek help, Allâh says: This is between Me and My slave. My slave will have whatever he has asked for. When the slave recites: Guide us to the straight path, the path of those on whom You bestowed Your favours. Those who neither exasperated you, nor went astray. At this, Allâh says: This is for My slave and My slave will have what he has asked for.

(This *Hadîth* is sound and reported by Muslim).

In the superiority of this opening chapter Ibn Taimiyah said: All the previous revelations (Books) were summarized in the three last Books; the Torah, the Psalms, and the Bible, these were in turn included in the Qur'ân, the Qur'ân was also summarized in the opening chapter. He added: It is an invocation, a prayer, a remembrance and it includes monotheism, servitude of Muslims to Allah عز وجل and it curses the Jews and the Christians who went astray. It is, to conclude, the best *Surah* of the Qur'ân – *Moqaddamatut-Tafseer.*

****

(٨٦) عَنْ أَبِي هُرَيرَةَ رَضِيَ اللهُ عَنْهُ عَنِ النَّبِيِّ ﷺ قَالَ: «إِنَّ اللهَ خَلَقَ الخَلْقَ حَتَّى إِذَا فَرَغَ مِنْ خَلْقِهِ قَالَتِ الرَّحِمُ هَذَا مَقَامُ الْعَائِذِ بِكَ مِنَ الْقَطِيعَةِ قَالَ: نَعَمْ أَمَا تَرْضِينَ أَنْ أَصِلَ مَنْ

وَصلَكِ وَأَقْطَعَ مَنْ قَطَعَكِ؟ قَالَتْ: بَلَى يَارَبِّ قَالَ: فَهُوَ لَكِ. قَالَ رَسُولُ اللهِ ﷺ: فَاقْرَءُوا إِنْ شِئْتُمْ ﴿فَهَلْ عَسَيْتُمْ إِنْ تَوَلَّيْتُمْ أَنْ تُفْسِدُوْا فِي الأَرْضِ وَتَقَطَّعُوْا أَرْحَامَكُمْ﴾».

«حديث صحيح» [رواه البخاري ومسلم]

Sin of breaking ties with the relatives

86) Narrated Abû Huraira رضى الله عنه: The Prophet صلى الله عليه وسلم said: Allâh created His creation and when he finished it, the womb said: This the place for him who seeks Your refuge from severing blood relationship. He said: Yes. Are you not satisfied that I should keep relationship with one who joins your ties (of relationship) and sever it with one who severs your ties. It said: Yes, O my Lord! He said: That is done for you. Allâh's Messenger صلى الله عليه وسلم said: Recite, if you wish, this verse:

> "Would you then, if you were given the authority, do mischief in the land, and sever your ties of kinship?" (47:22)

The Qur'ân always asserts the family connections, blood relations and the rights of the parents over all other rights. Blood relations should therefore be highly respected and maintained at all times. If you do every good deed and cut the womb relations, you may not be allowed to enter Paradise!

****

(٨٧) عَنْ أَبِي ذَرٍّ رَضِيَ اللهُ عَنْهُ عَنِ النَّبِيِّ ﷺ فِيمَا رُوِيَ عَنِ اللهِ تَبَارَكَ وَتَعَالَى أَنَّهُ قَالَ: «يَاعِبَادِي إِنِّي حَرَّمْتُ الظُّلْمَ عَلَى نَفْسِي وَجَعَلْتُهُ بَيْنَكُمْ مُحَرَّمًا فَلاَ تَظَالَمُوا، يَاعِبَادِي كُلُّكُمْ

ضَالٌّ إِلاَّ مَنْ هَدَيْتُهُ فَاسْتَهْدُوْنِي أَهْدِكُمْ، يَاعِبَادِي كُلُّكُمْ جَائِعٌ إِلاَّ مَنْ أَطْعَمْتُهُ فَاسْتَطْعَمُوْنِي أُطْعِمُكُمْ، يَاعِبَادِي كُلُّكُمْ عَارٍ إِلاَّ مَنْ كَسَوْتُهُ فَاسْتَكْسُونِي أَكْسُكُمْ، يَاعِبَادِي إِنَّكُمْ تُخْطِئُوْنَ بِاللَّيْلِ وَالنَّهَارِ وَأَنَا أَغْفِرُ الذُّنُوْبَ جَمِيْعًا فَاسْتَغْفِرُوْنِي أَغْفِرْلَكُمْ، يَاعِبَادِي إِنَّكُمْ لَنْ تَبْلُغُوا ضَرِّيْ فَتَضُرُّوْنِي وَلَنْ تَبْلُغُوا نَفْعِي فَتَنْفَعُوْنِي، يَاعِبَادِي لَوْ أَنَّ أَوَّلَكُمْ وَآخِرَكُمْ وَإِنْسَكُمْ وَجِنَّكُمْ كَانُوا عَلَى أَتْقَى قَلْبِ رَجُلٍ وَاحِدٍ مِنْكُمْ مَازَادَ ذَلِكَ فِي مُلْكِي شَيْئًا، يَاعِبَادِي لَوْ أَنَّ أَوَّلَكُمْ وَآخِرَكُمْ وَإِنْسَكُمْ وَجِنَّكُمْ كَانُوْا عَلَى أَفْجَرِ قَلْبِ رَجُلٍ وَاحِدٍ مَا نَقَصَ ذَلِكَ مِنْ مُلْكِي شَيْئًا، يَاعِبَادِيْ لَوْ أَنَّ أَوَّلَكُمْ وَآخِرَكُمْ وَإِنْسَكُمْ وَجِنَّكُمْ قَامُوا فِي صَعِيْدٍ وَاحِدٍ فَسَأَلُونِي فَأَعْطَيْتُ كُلَّ إِنْسَانٍ مَسْأَلَتَهُ مَا نَقَصَ ذٰلِكَ مِمَّا عِنْدِي إِلاَّ كَمَا يَنْقُصُ المِخْيَطُ إِذَا أُدْخِلَ الْبَحْرَ، يَاعِبَادِي إِنَّمَا هِيَ أَعْمَالُكُمْ أَحْصِيْهَا لَكُمْ ثُمَّ أُوَفِّيْكُمْ إِيَّاهَا فَمَنْ وَجَدَ خَيْرًا فَلْيَحْمَدِ اللهَ، وَمَنْ وَجَدَ غَيْرَ ذٰلِكَ فَلاَ يَلُوْمَنَّ إِلاَّ نَفْسَهُ». «حديث صحيح» [رواه مسلم]

Injustice is forbidden

87) Narrated Abû-Dhar رضى الله عنه: The Prophet صلى الله عليه وسلم said that Allâh تبارك وتعالى said: O My slaves! I have forbidden

injustice for Myself, so it is forbidden amongst you. So, do not be unjust to each other. O My slave! All of you are liable to go astray except the one whom I guide on the right path. So (always) seek guidance from Me, I will guide you. O My slave! All of you are hungry except the one whom I feed. So ask Me for food. I shall feed you. O My slave! All of you are naked except the one whom I make wear. So ask Me to make you wear and I shall make you wear. O My slave! You commit mistakes (sins) by day and night; and I forgive all the sins. So ask Me forgiveness, I shall forgive you (your sins). O My slaves! You will not attain harming Me so as to harm Me, and you will not attain benefiting Me so as to benefit Me. O My slaves! Were the first of you and the last of you, the human being of you and the jinn of you to be as pious as the most pious heart of any one of you, that would not increase My kingdom anything. O My slaves! Were the first of you and the last of you, the human of you and the jinn of you to be as wicked as the most wicked heart of any one of you, that would not decrease My kingdom anything. O My slaves! Were the first of you, the last of you, the human of you and the jinn of you to rise up in any place and make a request to Me and I have to give every one what he requested, that would not decrease what I have, anything more than a needle decreases the sea if it is put into it. O My slaves! Rather it is but your deeds which I will reckon for you, and then recompense for. So let, who finds good, praise Allâh and let, who finds other than that, blame no one but himself.

(This *Hadîth* is sound and reported by Muslim).

Injustice is one of the most bad qualities most widely practised among men since the dawn of history. Allah عز وجل made it *Haram* (unacceptable) and whoever practises injustice cannot be a good Muslim. Allah عز وجل Who is All-Judicious and All-Just wants us all, to practise every justice among ourselves.

****

(٨٨) عَنْ أَبِي هُرَيرَةَ رَضِيَ اللهُ عَنْهُ قَالَ: سَمِعْتُ النَّبِيَّ ﷺ يَقُولُ: «قَالَ اللهُ عَزَّ وَجَلَّ: وَمَنْ أَظْلَمُ مِمَّنْ ذَهَبَ يَخْلُقُ كَخَلْقِي فَلْيَخْلُقُوا ذَرَّةً أَوْ لِيَخْلُقُوا حَبَّةً أَوْ شَعِيْرَةً».

«حديث صحيح» [رواه البخاري ومسلم]

Portraying animateness is Forbidden

88) Narrated Abû Huraira رضى الله عنه: I heard the Prophet صلى الله عليه وسلم saying: Allâh عز وجل said: Who will be more transgressor than the one who tries to create the like of My creatures. Let him create an atom or let him create a grain or a barley seed.

(This *Hadîth* is sound and reported by Bukhâri and Muslim).

Scholars since old times have judged drawing and painting animate creatures unacceptable in Islam as per this *Hadith*, however, they have exempted photography of people for necessary purposes such as passports and I.Ds. As for photography or portraits for memory these are not allowed.

****

(٨٩) عَنْ أَبِي هُرَيرَةَ رَضِيَ اللهُ عَنْهُ قَالَ: قَالَ رَسُولُ اللهِ ﷺ: «تُفْتَحُ أَبْوَابُ الْجَنَّةِ فِي كُلِّ اثْنَيْنِ وَخَمِيْسَ فَيَغْفِرُ اللهُ عَزَّ وَجَلَّ لِكُلِّ عَبْدٍ لاَ يُشْرِكُ بِهِ شَيْئًا إِلاَّ الْمُتَشَاحِنَيْنِ يَقُوْلُ اللهُ لِلْمَلاَئِكَةِ ذَرُوْهُمَا حَتَّى يَصْطَلِحَا». «حديث حسن»

[رواه مسند أحمد]

Punishment of those who quarrel with one another

89) Narrated Abû Huraira رضى الله عنه: Allâh's Messenger صلى الله عليه وسلم said: Every Monday and Thursday, the gates of Paradise are open. Allâh عز وجل forgives every slave who associates no name in worship with Him except those who quarrelled with one another. Allâh says to the angels: Leave them until they reconcile.

(This *Hadîth* is good and reported by Ahmad in his *Musnad*).

As you may understand from this *Hadith*, if you quarrel with a Muslim you have to reconcile within three days. If you go on abandoning him, this is a great sin that prevents reward for even your good deeds until you have reconciled.

****

(٩٠) عَنْ أَبِي سَعِيْدٍ الخُدْرِيِّ رَضِيَ اللهُ عَنْهُ قَالَ: قَالَ رَسُولُ اللهِ ﷺ: «يُدْعَى نُوْحٌ يَوْمَ الْقِيَامَةِ فَيَقُوْلُ لَبَّيْكَ وَسَعْدَيْكَ يَارَبِّ فَيَقُوْلُ: هَلْ بَلَّغْتَ؟ فَيَقُوْلُ: نَعَمْ فَيُقَالُ لأُمَّتِهِ هَلْ بَلَّغَكُمْ؟ فَيَقُوْلُونَ: مَا أَتَانَا مِنْ نَذِيرٍ فَيَقُوْلُ: مَنْ يَشْهَدُ لَكَ؟ فَيَقُوْلُ: مُحَمَّدٌ وَأُمَّتُهُ فَيَشْهَدُوْنَ أَنَّهُ قَدْ بَلَّغَ، وَيَكُوْنُ الرَّسُوْلُ عَلَيْكُمْ شَهِيْدًا فَذٰلِكَ قَوْلُ اللهِ عَزَّ وَجَلَّ ذِكْرُهُ ﴿وَكَذٰلِكَ جَعَلْنَاكُمْ أُمَّةً وَسَطًا لِّتَكُوْنُوا شُهَدَاءَ عَلَى النَّاسِ وَيَكُوْنَ الرَّسُولُ عَلَيْكُمْ شَهِيْدًا﴾» . «حديث صحيح» [رواه البخاري والترمذي وابن ماجه]

Superiority of the Followers of Muhammad صلى الله عليه وسلم

90) Narrated Abû Sa'îd Al-Khudri رضى الله عنه: Allâh's Messenger صلى الله عليه وسلم said: On the Day of Resurrection, Nûh (عليه السلام) will be called. He will say: I do respond and am at Your pleasure, O Lord! Allâh will ask: Did you convey Our Message of Monotheism to your people? Nûh will say: Yes. Then his nation will be asked: Did he convey the Divine Message to you? They will say: No warner came to us. Allâh will say to Nûh (عليه السلام) : Who will bear witness in your favour? He will say: Muhammad (صلى الله عليه وسلم) and his followers. So they will all testify that he had conveyed the (Divine) Message (to his people). And the Messenger will also be a witness to you according to the Statement of Allâh (عز و جل):

> "Thus We have made you [true Muslims – real believers of Islâmic Monotheism, true followers of Prophet Muhammad صلى الله عليه وسلم and his *Sunnah* (legal ways)], a just (and the best) nation, that you be witnesses over mankind and the Messenger (Muhammad صلى الله عليه وسلم) will be witness upon you". (2:143)

(This *Hadîth* is sound and reported by Bukhâri, Tirmidhi and Ibn Mâjah).

Once Muhammad صلى الله عليه وسلم is the most honoured Prophet, his nation (*Ummah*) is eventually the best *Ummah* that will enter Paradise first. In other words, they are the last Prophet's nation, but the first to enter Paradise. They are privileged, unlike the previous *Ummah* e.g. a sin of Muhammad's *Ummah* is counted one, but a virtue is counted ten for them.

****

(٩١) عَنْ أَنَسِ بْنِ مَالِكٍ رَضِيَ اللهُ عَنْهُ أَنَّ رَسُولَ اللهِ ﷺ قَالَ: «أَتَانِي جِبْرِيلُ بِمِثْلِ هَذِهِ الْمِرْآةِ الْبَيْضَاءِ فِيْهَا نُكْتَةٌ سَوْدَاء قُلْتُ يَاجِبْرِيْلُ مَا هَذِهِ؟ قَالَ هَذِهِ الْجُمُعَةُ جَعَلَهَا اللهُ عِيْدًا لَكَ وَلِأُمَّتِكَ فَأَنْتُمْ قَبْلَ الْيَهُوْدِ وَالنَّصَارَى، فِيْهَا سَاعَةٌ لاَ يُوَافِقُهَا عَبْدٌ يَسْأَلُ اللهَ فِيْهَا خَيْرًا إِلاَّ أَعْطَاهُ إِيَّاهُ قَالَ: قُلْتُ مَا هَذِهِ النُّكْتَةُ السَّوْدَاء؟ قَالَ هَذَا يَوْمُ الْقِيَامَةِ تَقُوْمُ فِي يَوْمِ الْجُمُعَةِ وَنَحْنُ نَدْعُوْهُ عِنْدَنَا الْمَزِيْدَ قَالَ قُلْتُ: مَا يَوْمُ الْمَزِيْدِ؟ قَالَ إِنَّ اللهَ جَعَلَ فِي الْجَنَّةِ وَادِيًا أَفْيَحَ وَجَعَلَ فِيْهِ كُثْبَانًا مِنَ الْمِسْكِ الأَبْيَضِ فَإِذَا كَانَ يَوْمُ الْجُمُعَةِ يَنْزِلُ اللهُ فِيْهِ فَوُضِعَتْ فِيْهِ مَنَابِرُ مِنْ ذَهَبٍ لِلأَنْبِيَاءِ وَكَرَاسِيُّ مِنْ دُرٍّ لِلشُّهَدَاءِ وَيَنْزِلْنَ الْحُوْرُ الْعِيْنُ مِنَ الْغُرَفِ فَحَمِدُوْا اللهَ وَمَجَّدُوْهُ قَالَ ثُمَّ يَقُوْلُ اللهُ: اُكْسُوْا عِبَادِي فَيُكْسَوْنَ وَيَقُوْلُ أَطْعِمُوْا عِبَادِي فَيُطْعَمُوْنَ وَيَقُوْلُ اِسْقُوْا عِبَادِي فَيُسْقَوْنَ وَيَقُوْلُ طَيِّبُوْا عِبَادِي فَيُطَيَّبُوْنَ ثُمَّ يَقُوْلُ مَاذَا تُرِيْدُوْنَ؟ فَيَقُوْلُوْنَ رَبَّنَا رِضْوَانَكَ قَالَ يَقُوْلُ: رَضِيْتُ عَنْكُمْ ثُمَّ يَأْمُرُهُمْ فَيَنْطَلِقُوْنَ وَتَصْعَدُ الْحُوْرُ الْعِيْنُ الْغُرَفَ وَهِيَ مِنْ زُمُرُّدَةٍ خَضْرَاءَ وَمِنْ يَاقُوْتَةٍ حَمْرَاءَ». «حديث صحيح» [رواه مسند أبي يعلى]

91) Narrated Anas bin Mâlik رضى الله عنه that Allâh's Messenger صلى الله عليه وسلم said: Once Jibrael brought me a white mirror having a black dot. So, I asked: O Jibrael! What is this? He said: This is Friday. Allâh has made it a festival for you and your followers. So you have been given preference more than the Jews and Christians. There is an hour on Friday nothing any slave ask is not answered. Then the Prophet صلى الله عليه وسلم said: I asked: What is this black spot? The angel replied: This is the Final Hour that will take place on a Friday. We call it "*Al-Mazid*". The Prophet صلى الله عليه وسلم said: I asked him: What is the hour of *Al-Mazid*? He said: Allâh has made in Paradise a wide valley in which He has created dunes of white musk. When it is Friday, Allâh will descend to it. The pulpits of gold are kept there for the Prophets and chairs made of pearl are arranged for the martyrs and the maidens with big lustrous eyes will get down from their upstair rooms. They all praise Allâh and glorify Him. The Prophet صلى الله عليه وسلم said: Then Allâh will say: Cloth My slaves. So they will be dressed. He will say: Feed My slaves. So they will be fed. He will say: Make them drink. So they will be made to drink. He will say: Perfume My slaves. So they will be perfumed. Then He will ask: What do you want? They will say: O our Lord! We want Your pleasure. The Prophet صلى الله عليه وسلم said: Allâh will say: I am pleased with you. Then He will order them to disperse. So they will deport. And the maidens with big lustrous eyes ascend to the upstair rooms, which are made of green emerald and red ruby.

(This *Hadîth* is sound and reported in *Musnad* of Abi Ya'la).

****

(٩٢) عَنْ أَصْحَابِ النَّبِيِّ ﷺ أَنَّ النَّبِيَّ ﷺ قَالَ: «يَرِدُ عَلَى

الْحَوْضِ رِجَالٌ مِنْ أَصْحَابِي فَيُحَلَّئُوْنَ عَنْهُ فَأَقُوْلُ يَارَبِّ أَصْحَابِي فَيَقُوْلُ: لاَ عِلْمَ لَكَ بِمَا أَحْدَثُوا بَعْدَكَ إِنَّهُمُ ارْتَدُّوْا عَلَى أَدْبَارِهِمُ الْقَهْقَرَى». «حديث صحيح» [رواه البخاري]

Punishment of the one who alters in religion after the death of the Prophet صلى الله عليه وسلم

92) Narrated the Companions of the Prophet صلى الله عليه وسلم that the Prophet صلى الله عليه وسلم said: Some people of my Companions will arrive at the cistern of my *Haud* (pool) but they will be turned away (from it). So I will say: O Lord! They are my Companions. He will say: You don't know what heterodoxy they made after (your death), and reverted.

(This *Hadîth* is sound and reported by Bukhâri).

This *Hadith* asserts the role of the *Sunnah* (Prophetic traditions: sayings, deeds, approvals, and qualities of Muhammad صلى الله عليه وسلم). Deviation from the Prophet's method is definitely going astray. One has to pray as he did, to invoke as he did, to sit as he did, to eat as he did, to smile as he did etc... Muhammad صلى الله عليه وسلم was the demonstrator who showed his Companions every thing even how to behave in the toilet, this means that he left for us a complete religion for all what one might need in his everyday life. So if you know the *Sunnah*, you have to apply it and if you do not know, you have to ask. Asking to know your religion is obligatory.

****

(٩٣) عَنْ عَبْدِ اللهِ بْنِ عَمْرِو بْنِ الْعَاصِ رَضِيَ اللهُ عَنْهُمَا أَنَّ النَّبِيَّ ﷺ تَلاَ قَوْلَ اللهِ عَزَّ وَجَلَّ فِي إِبْرَاهِيمَ ﴿رَبِّ إِنَّهُنَّ أَضْلَلْنَ كَثِيْرًا مِنَ النَّاسِ فَمَنْ تَبِعَنِي فَإِنَّهُ مِنِّي﴾ وَقَالَ عِيْسَى عَلَيْهِ السَّلاَمُ

﴿إِنْ تُعَذِّبْهُمْ فَإِنَّهُمْ عِبَادُكَ، وَإِنْ تَغْفِرْ لَهُمْ فَإِنَّكَ أَنْتَ الْعَزِيْزُ الْحَكِيْمُ﴾ فَرَفَعَ يَدَيْهِ وَقَالَ: اللَّهُمَّ أُمَّتِي أُمَّتِي وَبَكَى فَقَالَ اللهُ عَزَّ وَجَلَّ يَاجِبْرِيْلُ اذْهَبْ إِلَى مُحَمَّدٍ - وَرَبُّكَ أَعْلَمُ - فَسَلْهُ مَا يُبْكِيْكَ، فَأَتَاهُ جِبْرِيْلُ عَلَيْهِ الصَّلاَةُ وَالسَّلاَمُ فَسَأَلَهُ فَأَخْبَرَهُ رَسُوْلُ اللهِ ﷺ بِمَا قَالَ - وَهُوَ أَعْلَمُ - فَقَالَ اللهُ: يَاجِبْرِيْلُ اذْهَبْ إِلَى مُحَمَّدٍ فَقُلْ إِنَّا سَنُرْضِيْكَ فِي أُمَّتِكَ وَلاَ نَسُوْءُكَ».

«حديث صحيح» [رواه مسلم]

93) Narrated 'Abdullâh bin Amr bin Al-Aas رضى الله عنهما that the Prophet صلى الله عليه وسلم recited the Words of Allâh عزوجل that Ibrâhim uttered: My Lord! They (the idols) - have misguided lots of people. So who follows me, is verily of me, and Jesus عليه السلام said: If you punish them, they are Your slaves. If You forgive them, You are the All-Mighty, the All-Wise. Then he raised his hands and said: O Allâh! My *Ummah*, (people) My *Ummah* and wept. So Allâh عزوجل said: O Jibrael! Go to Muhammad - though your Lord knows best - and ask him: What makes you weep? So Jibrael عليه الصلاة و السلام came to him and asked him (about the matter). Allâh's Messenger صلى الله عليه وسلم informed him of what he had said - though Allâh knows best. When Jibrael reported to Allâh, He said: O Jibrael! Go back to Muhammad and say: We will please you with regard to your *Ummah* and We will not cause you any harm.

(This *Hadîth* is sound and reported by Muslim).

****

(٩٤) عَنْ أَبِي أُمَامَةَ قَالَ: قَالَ رَسُولُ اللهِ ﷺ: «يَاابْنَ آدَمَ إِنَّكَ إِنْ تَبْذُلِ الْفَضْلَ خَيْرٌ لَكَ، وَإِنْ تُمْسِكْهُ شَرٌّ لَكَ وَلاَ تُلاَمُ عَلَى كَفَافٍ، وَابْدَأْ بِمَنْ تَعُوْلُ، وَالْيَدُ الْعُلْيَا خَيْرٌ مِنَ الْيَدِ السُّفْلَى». «حديث صحيح» [رواه مسلم]

The Upper Hand is better than the Lower

94) Abû Umama narrated that the Prophet صلى الله عليه وسلم said: O son of Adam if you do good (spend), it is better and if you do not spend that is bad for you. But if you are poor; no blame. Start with (when you spend) your dependents. The Prophet added: The upper hand is better than the lower.

(This *Hadith* is sound and reported by Muslim).

A giving (spending) hand is definitely better than the beggar's (the lower).

****

(٩٥) عَنِ ابْنِ عَبَّاسٍ رَضِيَ اللهُ عَنْهُمَا قَالَ: قَالَ رَسُولِ اللهِ ﷺ: «سَأَلْتُ رَبِّي مَسْأَلَةً وَدِدْتُ أَنِّي لَمْ أَسْأَلْهُ، قُلْتُ: يَارَبِّ كَانَتْ قَبْلِي رُسُلٌ مِنْهُمْ مَنْ سَخَّرْتَ لَهُمُ الرِّيَاحَ، وَمِنْهُمْ مَنْ كَانَ يُحْيِي الْمَوْتَى. قَالَ: أَلَمْ أَجِدْكَ يَتِيمًا فَآوَيْتُكَ؟ أَلَمْ أَجِدْكَ ضَالاً فَهَدَيْتُكَ؟ أَلَمْ أَجِدْكَ عَائِلاً فَأَغْنَيْتُكَ؟ أَلَمْ أَشْرَحْ لَكَ صَدْرَكَ؟ وَوَضَعْتُ عَنْكَ وِزْرَكَ؟ قَالَ: قُلْتُ بَلَى يَارَبِّ».

«حديث حسن» [الطبراني في المعجم الكبير]

Allâh's Endowment upon Prophet Muhammad صلى الله عليه و سلم

95) Ibn Abbas رضى الله عنه narrated that the Prophet صلى الله عليه وسلم said: I asked Allâh something I wish I had not. I said: O Lord there were some Prophets before me. You made the wind yield to one of them and one could make the dead alive (by Your bounty). The Prophet صلى الله عليه وسلم said: Allâh said to me: Did I not find you an orphan (O Muhammad) and give you refuge. Did I not find you unaware (of the Qur'ân) and guide you. Did I not find you poor and make you rich? Did I not take off you, your burden? The Prophet صلى الله عليه وسلم said: Yes, My Lord.

(This *Hadîth* is good and reported by At-Tabarâni in his *Al-Mu'jam Al-Kabeer).*

It is enough that Prophet Muhammad صلى الله عليه وسلم is the most honourable Prophet. Though, he was given a lot of qualities no other Prophet ever had had, e.g. intercession on Doomsday. His *Ummah* is also the best and the first to enter Paradise.

****

(٩٦) عَنْ أَنَسٍ أَنَّ النَّبِيَّ ﷺ قَالَ اللهُ تَعَالَى: «مَا مِنْ مُسْلِمٍ يَمُوتُ فَيَشْهَدُ لَهُ أَرْبَعَةُ أَهْلِ أَبْيَاتٍ مِنْ جِيرَانِهِ الأَدْنَيْنَ إِلا قَالَ الله تعالى: قَدْ قَبِلْتُ عِلْمَكُمْ فِيهِ وَغَفَرْتُ لَهُ مَا لا تَعْلَمُونَ».

«حسن لغيره» [رواه أحمد والحاكم في المستدرك]

If neighbours witness that the dead was pious Allâh forgives him

96) Anas رضى الله عنه narrated that the Prophet صلى الله عليه و سلم said: If any Muslim dies and four of his closest neighbours witness that he was pious, Allâh says: I approve what you

know about him, and forgive him (what you do not know).

(This *Hadîth* is fairly good and reported by Ahmad and Al-Hâkim).

People are the witnesses of Allâh in this world. What all Muslims agree upon is very often right.

****

(٩٧) عَنْ أَبِي هُرَيرَةَ عَنِ النَّبِيِّ ﷺ أَنَّهُ قَالَ ـ يَعْنِي الله تَبَارَكَ وَتَعَالَى ـ : «لاَ يَنْبَغِي لِعَبْدٍ لِي ﴿وَقَالَ ابْنُ الْمُثَنَّى : لِعَبْدِي﴾ أَنْ يَقُوْلَ : أَنَا خَيْرٌ مِنْ يُوْنُسَ بْنَ مَتَّى عَلَيْهِ السَّلاَمُ» .

«حديث صحيح» [رواه مسلم والبخاري]

97) Abû Huraira narrated: Prophet Muhammad صلى الله عليه و سلم said: Allâh said: Any slave of mine (Ibn Muthanna narrated Allâh said: My slave) ought not claim to be better than Yunus (Jonah عليه السلام), the son of Metta.

(This *Hadith* is sound and reported by Bukhâri and Muslim).

No believer can claim to be better than Yunus عليه السلام, but other Prophets (peace be upon them) can and among them Muhammad صلى الله عليه وسلم is the most honourable.

****

(٩٨) عَنْ عُتْبَةَ بْنِ عَبْدٍ السَّلْمِيِّ عَنِ النَّبِيِّ ﷺ قَالَ : «يَأْتِي الشُّهَدَاءُ وَالْمُتَوَفُّوْنَ بِالطَّاعُوْنِ فَيَقُوْلُ أَصْحَابُ الطَّاعُوْنِ : نَحْنَ شُهَدَاءُ فَيُقَالُ : انْظُرُوْا فَإِنْ كَانَتْ جِرَاحُهُمْ كَجِرَاحِ الشُّهَدَاءِ

تَسِيْلُ دَمًا رِيْحَ الْمِسْكِ فَهُمْ شُهَدَاءُ فَيَجِدُوْنَهُمْ كَذَلِكَ».

«حديث حسن» [رواه مسند أحمد]

The Plague Reward

98) Utba Ibn Abd As-Salami narrated that Prophet Muhammad صلى الله عليه و سلم said: Martyrs and who died of plague will come (on Doomsday). The ones who died of plague will say: We are the martyrs. Then it will be said: See if their wounds look like those of the martyrs bleeding and smelling as musk, they are (really) martyrs. They will prove so upon smelling.

(This *Hadîth* is good and reported by Ahmad in his *Musnad*).

Martyrs in the nation (*Ummah*) of the Prophet صلى الله عليه وسلم are not merely who die while fighting in the cause of Allâh, but they also include people who die of plague, and many others.

****

(٩٩) عَنْ مُحَمَّدِ بْنِ جُبَيْرِ بْنِ مُطْعَمٍ عَنْ أَبِيهِ: أَنَّ رَجُلاً أَتَى النَّبِيَّ ﷺ فَقَالَ: يَارَسُوْلَ اللهِ أَيُّ الْبُلْدَانِ شَرٌّ؟ قَالَ: فَقَالَ: «لاَ أَدْرِي، فَلَمَّا أَتَاهُ جِبْرِيلُ عَلَيْهِ السَّلاَمُ قَالَ: يَاجِبْرِيلُ أَيُّ الْبُلْدَانِ شَرٌّ؟ قَالَ: لاَ أَدْرِي حَتَّى أَسْأَلَ رَبِّي عَزَّ وَجَلَّ، فَانْطَلَقَ جِبْرِيلُ عَلَيْهِ السَّلاَمُ ثُمَّ مَكَثَ مَا شَاءَ اللهُ أَنْ يَمْكُثَ ثُمَّ جَاءَ فَقَالَ: يَا مُحَمَّدُ إِنَّكَ سَأَلْتَنِي أَيُّ الْبُلْدَانِ شَرٌّ؟ فَقُلْتُ: لاَ أَدْرِي وَإِنِّي سَأَلْتُ رَبِّي عَزَّ وَجَلَّ أَيُّ الْبُلْدَانِ شَرٌّ؟ فَقَالَ: أَسْوَاقُهَا».

«حسن لغيره» [رواه أحمد والحاكم في المستدرك والطبراني]

The Worst Places

99) Muhammad bin Jubair bin Mut'am narrated that somebody came to the Prophet صلى الله عليه و سلم and asked him: What are the worst places? The Prophet صلى الله عليه و سلم answered: I do not know. Then Jibrael (عليه السلام) came to the Prophet صلى الله عليه و سلم and was asked by the Prophet what are the worst places? Jibrael (عليه السلام) said: I do not know, but I will ask my Lord . Jibrael left and was away as much as Allâh wished, then came to the Prophet صلى الله عليه وسلم and said: O Muhammad, you asked me what are the worst places and once I did not know I asked Allâh سبحانه و تعالى and He said: (These are) the markets.

(This *Hadîth* is fairly good and reported by Ahmad in his *Musnad*, Al-Hâkim in his *Mustadrak* and At-Tabarâni in the big *Mu'jam*).

This *Hadîth* shows us that markets and shopping areas are worst places because they are where people chase worldly pleasures and money. Some people do not follow the commands of the Noble Qur'ân and the sound *Sunnah*. They just want to get money or pleasure, no matter if it is acceptable in Islâm or not. But a true Muslim should always consult the Noble Qur'ân and the *Sunnah* of Prophet Muhammad صلى الله عليه و سلم.

****

(١٠٠) عَنْ أَنَسٍ قَالَ: بَيْنَا رَسُولُ اللهِ ﷺ ذَاتَ يَوْمٍ بَيْنَ أَظْهُرِنَا إِذَا أَغْفَى إِغْفَاءَةً ثُمَّ رَفَعَ رَأْسَهُ مُبْتَسِمًا، فَقُلْنَا: مَا أَضْحَكَكَ يارسول الله! قال: «أُنْزِلَتْ عَلَيَّ آنِفًا سُورَةٌ فَقَرَأَ: بِسْمِ اللهِ الرَّحْمٰنِ الرَّحِيمِ ﴿إِنَّا أَعْطَيْنَاكَ الْكَوْثَرَ، فَصَلِّ لِرَبِّكَ وَانْحَرْ، إِنَّ شَانِئَكَ هُوَ الأَبْتَرُ﴾ ثُمَّ قَالَ: أَتَدْرُوْنَ مَا الْكَوْثَرُ؟

فَقُلْنَا : اللهُ وَرَسُوْلُهُ أَعْلَمُ قَالَ : فَإِنَّهُ نَهْرٌ وَعَدَنِيْهِ رَبِّي عَزَّ وَجَلَّ عَلَيْهِ خَيْرٌ كَثِيْرٌ هُوَ حَوْضٌ تَرِدُ عَلَيْهِ أُمَّتِي يَوْمَ الْقِيَامَةِ آنِيَتُهُ عَدَدُ النُّجُوْمِ فَيُخْتَلَجُ العَبْدُ مِنْهُمْ فَأَقُوْلُ : رَبِّ إِنَّهُ مِنْ أُمَّتِي فَيَقُوْلُ : مَا تَدْرِي مَا أَحْدَثُو بَعْدَكَ» . «حديث صحيح»

[رواه مسلم وأبو داؤود والنسائي]

The *Kauthar* (a river of Prophet Muhammad صلى الله عليه و سلم in Paradise)

100) Anas رضي الله عنه narrated: Prophet Muhammad صلى الله عليه و سلم one day took a nap among us and woke up laughing. We asked him: O Messenger of Allâh, why did you smile. The Prophet صلى الله عليه وسلم said: A *Surah* was revealed to me before. Then he read out :"In the Name of Allâh, the Most Beneficent, the Most Merciful":

> "Verily, We have granted you (O Muhammad) *Al-Kauthar* (a river in Paradise). Therefore, turn in prayer to your Lord and sacrifice (to Him only). For, he who makes you angry (O Muhammad) will be cut off " (*Sweat Al-Kauthar*)

Then the Prophet صلى الله عليه وسلم asked: Do you know what *Al-Kauthar* is? The narrator said we said: Allâh and His Messenger know best. Then the Prophet صلى الله عليه وسلم said: It is a river in Paradise Allâh pledged to give me. It is full of every thing good and my *Ummah* will aim at it on the Day of Resurrection. Its cups are as many as stars. Some of my followers will be prevented from it and I will ask O my Lord they are my followers. Allâh will say: You (O Muhammad) do not know how they took to heterodoxy after you).

(This *Hadîth* is sound and reported by Muslim, Abû Dâ'ud and Nas'ai).

This *Hadîth* reflects the danger of deviation from the *Sunnah* of the Prophet صلى الله عليه وسلم. Every good deed has two conditions to be accepted by Allâh: One is that it should be done solely for Allâh without any partner whatsoever. Second condition is that it should be performed according to the *Sunnah*, i.e. tradition of the Prophet صلى الله عليه وسلم.

****

(١٠١) عَنْ عَبْدِ اللهِ بْنِ عَمْرِو بْنِ العَاصِ رَضِيَ اللهُ عَنْهُمَا قَالَ: قَالَ رَسُولُ اللهِ ﷺ: «إِنَّ اللهَ سَيُخَلِّصُ رَجُلاً مِنْ أُمَّتِي عَلَى رُؤُوسِ الخَلاَئِقِ يَوْمَ القِيَامَةِ فَيَنْشُرُ عَلَيْهِ تِسْعَةً وَتِسْعِيْنَ سِجِلاًّ كُلُّ سِجِلٍّ مِثْلُ مَدِّ الْبَصَرِ ثُمَّ يَقُولُ: أَتُنْكِرُ مِنْ هَذَا شَيْئًا؟ أَظَلَمَكَ كَتَبَتِي الحَافِظُوْنَ؟ فَيَقُولُ: لاَ يَارَبِّ. فَيَقُولُ أَفَلَكَ عُذْرٌ؟ فَيَقُوْلُ: لاَ يَارَبِّ فَيَقُوْلُ: بَلَى إِنَّ لَكَ عِنْدَنَا حَسَنَةً فَإِنَّهُ لاَ ظُلْمَ عَلَيْكَ اليَوْمَ. فَتُخْرَجُ بِطَاقَةٌ فِيْهَا أَشْهَدُ أَنْ لاَ إِلَهَ إِلاَّ اللهُ وَأَشْهَدُ أَنَّ مُحَمَّدًا عَبْدُهُ وَرَسُوْلُهُ فَيَقُولُ: أَحْضِرْ وَزْنَكَ فَيَقُولُ: يَارَبِّ مَا هَذِهِ البِطَاقَةُ مَعَ هَذِهِ السِّجِلاَّتِ فَقَالَ: إِنَّكَ لاَ تُظْلَمُ قَالَ: فَتُوْضَعُ السِّجِلاَّتُ فِي كَفَّةٍ وَالبِطَاقَةُ فِي كَفَّةٍ فَطَاشَتِ السِّجِلاَّتُ وَثَقُلَتِ البِطَاقَةُ فَلاَ يَثْقُلُ مَعَ اسْمِ اللهِ شَيْءٌ».

«حديث صحيح»

[رواه الترمذي وابن ماجه ومسند أحمد]

Superiority of the words لا اله الا الله (There is no God but Allâh)

101) Narrated by 'Abdullâh bin Amr bin Al-'Aas رضى الله عنه that Allâh's Messenger صلى الله عليه وسلم said: On the Day of Resurrection, Allâh will bring a person of my *Ummah* from among the people; and spread before him ninety-nine registers (filled up with his deeds). Each of them will be as long as sight extends. Then Allâh will ask him: Do you deny anything of it? Have My preserving writers treated you unjustly? The person will reply: No, my Lord. Allâh will further ask him: Do you have any excuse (for not having good deeds)? He will say: No, my Lord. Then Allâh will observe: Behold! We have preserved a virtue of yours with us. Today there will be no wrong with you. Then Allâh will take out a slip containing the words: "There is no God but Allâh and that Muhammad is His slave and Messenger"; and Allah will address the person: Bring up your weights (of this slip). The person will remark: O Lord! This slip (is so light in weight) that it may not be matched with these large registers. Allâh will observe: You will be done no injustice. The Prophet صلى الله عليه وسلم added: All the registers will be piled up in one scale and the slip will be kept in the other scale of the balance. (With the Grace of Allâh), the scale with the registers will be raised up (due to light weight) while the scale having the slip will be the heavier as there is nothing that weighs more than the Name of Allâh.

(This *Hadîth* is sound and reported by Tirmidhi, Ibn Mâjah and Ahmad in his *Musnad*).

This above *Hadith* briefly describes that Allah, if He likes, can forgive even the most sinner person believing in Oneness of Allah and the Prophethood of Muhammad صلى الله عليه وسلم. But it doesn't mean that every one should take it as a cover and involve himself intentionally in evils relying on the Mercy of

Allah. A good Muslim who has in his heart fear of Allah, should perform righteous deeds and avoid sins as per commands laid down in the Qur'ân and *Hadith.*

****

(١٠٢) عَنِ ابْنِ عَبَّاسٍ رَضِيَ اللهُ عَنْهُمَا قَالَ: لَمَّا نَزَلَتْ هٰذِهِ الآيَةُ ﴿وَإِنْ تُبْدُوْا مَا فِي أَنْفُسِكُمْ أَوْ تُخْفُوهُ يُحَاسِبْكُمْ بِهِ اللهُ﴾ قَالَ: دَخَلَ قُلُوْبَهُمْ مِنْهَا شَيْءٌ، لَمْ يَدْخُلْ قُلُوبَهُمْ مِنْ شَيْءٍ فَقَالَ النَّبِيُّ ﷺ: «قُوْلُوا سَمِعْنَا وَأَطَعْنَا وَسَلَّمْنَا» قَالَ: فَأَلْقَى اللهُ الإِيْمَانَ فِي قُلُوْبِهِمْ فَأَنْزَلَ اللَّهُ تَعَالَى ﴿لاَ يُكَلِّفُ اللَّهُ نَفْسًا إِلاَّ وُسْعَهَا لَهَا مَاكَسَبَتْ وَعَلَيْهَا مَااكْتَسَبَتْ رَبَّنَا لاَتُؤَاخِذْنَا إِنْ نَسِيْنَا أَوْ أَخْطَأْنَا﴾ قَالَ: قَدْ فَعَلْتُ ﴿رَبَّنَا وَلاَتُحَمِّلْ عَلَيْنَا إِصْرًا كَمَا حَمَلْتَهُ عَلَى الَّذِيْنَ مِنْ قَبْلِنَا﴾ قَالَ: قَدْ فَعَلْتُ ﴿وَاغْفِرْ لَنَا وَارْحَمْنَا أَنْتَ مَوْلاَنَا﴾ [البقرة : ٢٨٦] قَالَ: قَدْ فَعَلْتُ. «حديث صحيح» [رواه مسلم وسنن الترمذي]

Statement of Allâh عز وجل : "Whether you disclose what is in your minds or conceal, Allâh will reckon you accordingly".

102) Ibn 'Abbâs رضى الله عنهما said: When this verse was revealed: "Whether you disclose what is in your minds or conceal it, Allâh will call you to account according to it". It caused anxiety to the Companions as had never been before. Then Allâh's Messenger صلى الله عليه وسلم observed:

Say: We have heard and obeyed and submitted (to the Lord!). The narrator added: Allâh instilled Faith in their hearts and further revealed (for their satisfaction) this verse: "Allâh burdens not a soul beyond its capacity. It will get every good that it earns and it will suffer every ill that it commits. Our Lord! Call us not to account if we forget or make a mistake". (When they said the same verse) Allâh said: I have done. They further said: Our Lord! Lay not upon us a burden as your did lay on those before us. Allah said: I have done so. The Companions further said: And pardon us, have Mercy on us. You are our Protector. The Lord said: Done.

(This *Hadîth* is sound and reported by Bukhâri and Tirmidhi).

****

(١٠٣) عَنْ أَبِي هُرَيْرَةَ رَضِيَ اللهُ عَنْهُ قَالَ: «لَمَّا نَزَلَتْ عَلَى رَسُوْلِ اللهِ ﷺ ﴿للهِ مَا فِي السَّمٰوَاتِ وَمَا فِي الأَرْضِ وَإِنْ تُبْدُوْا ما فِي أَنْفُسِكُمْ أَوْ تُخْفُوْهُ يُحَاسِبْكُمْ بِهِ اللهُ فَيَغْفِرُ لِمَنْ يَّشَاءُ وَيُعَذِّبُ مَنْ يَّشَاءُ وَاللهُ عَلَى كُلِّ شَيْءٍ قَدِيْرٌ﴾ قَالَ فَاشْتَدَّ ذَلِكَ عَلَى أَصْحَابِ رَسُوْلِ اللهِ ﷺ فَأَتَوْا رَسُوْلَ اللهِ ﷺ ثُمَّ بَرَكُوا عَلَى الرُّكَبِ فَقَالُوا: أَيْ رَسُولَ اللهِ! كُلِّفْنَا مِنَ الأَعْمَالِ مَا نُطِيْقُ اَلصَّلاَةُ وَالصِّيَامُ وَالْجِهَادُ وَالصَّدَقَةُ، وَقَدْ أُنْزِلَتْ عَلَيْكَ هَذِهِ الآيَةُ وَلاَنُطِيْقُهَا قَالَ رَسُوْلُ اللَّهِ ﷺ: «أَتُرِيْدُوْنَ أَنْ تَقُولُوا كَمَا قَالَ أَهْلُ الْكِتَابَيْنِ مِنْ قَبْلِكُمْ سَمِعْنَا وَعَصَيْنَا؟ بَلْ قُوْلُوا

سَمِعْنَا وَأَطَعْنَا غُفْرَانَكَ رَبَّنَا وَإِلَيْكَ الْمَصِيْرُ» قَالُوا: سَمِعْنَا
وَأَطَعْنَا غُفْرَانَكَ رَبَّنَا وَإِلَيْكَ الْمَصِيْرُ فَلَمَّا اقْتَرَأَهَا الْقَوْمُ ذَلَّتْ
بِهَا أَلْسِنَتُهُمْ فَأَنْزَلَ اللَّهُ فِي إِثْرِهَا ﴿آمَنَ الرَّسُوْلُ بِمَا أُنْزِلَ إِلَيْهِ
مِنْ رَبِّهِ وَالْمُؤْمِنُوْنَ، كُلٌّ آمَنَ بِاللهِ وَمَلاَئِكَتِهِ وَكُتُبِهِ وَرُسُلِهِ
لاَنُفَرِّقُ بَيْنَ أَحَدٍ مِنْ رُسُلِهِ، وَقَالُوْا سَمِعْنَا وَأَطَعْنَا غُفْرَانَكَ
رَبَّنَا وَإِلَيْكَ الْمَصِيْرُ﴾ فَلَمَّا فَعَلُوْا ذَلِكَ نَسَخَهَا اللهُ تَعَالَى فَأَنْزَلَ
اللهُ عَزَّ وَجَلَّ ﴿لاَيُكَلِّفُ اللهُ نَفْسًا إِلاَّ وُسْعَهَا لَهَا مَا كَسَبَتْ
وَعَلَيْهَا مَا اكْتَسَبَتْ، رَبَّنَا لاَتُؤَاخِذْنَا إِنْ نَسِيْنَا أَوْ أَخْطَأْنَا﴾
قَالَ: نَعَمْ ﴿رَبَّنَا وَلاَ تُحَمِّلْنَا مَالاَ طَاقَةَ لَنَا بِهِ﴾ قَالَ: نَعَمْ
﴿وَاعْفُ عَنَّا وَاغْفِرْ لَنَا وَارْحَمْنَا أَنْتَ مَوْلاَنَا فَانْصُرْنَا عَلَى
الْقَوْمِ الْكَافِرِيْنَ﴾ قَالَ: نَعَمْ. «حديث صحيح» [رواه مسلم]

103) Narrated Abû Huraira رضى الله عنه: When this verse was revealed to Allâh's Messenger صلى الله عليه وسلم: "To Allâh belongs whatever is in the heavens and whatever is in the earth and whether you disclose what is in your minds or conceal it, Allâh will reckon you according to it. Then He will forgive whom He pleases and chastise whom He likes as Allâh is All-Omnipotent over every thing." The narrator said: The Companions of Allâh's Messenger صلى الله عليه وسلم felt it hard. They came to him, sat down on their knees and said: O Messenger of Allâh, we have been assigned with some duties (tasks) which we have capability to perform such as: prayer (*Salât*), fasting (*Saum*), fighting in Allâh's

way (*Jihâd*), and charity (*Zakat*). Now this (the above mentioned verse) was revealed to you and it is beyond our power to live up to. Then Allâh's Messenger صلى الله عليه وسلم said: Do you intend to say what the people of the two Scriptures (the Jews and Christians) had said before you: "We hear and disobey". Rather you should say: "We hear, obey and seek your forgiveness, our Lord! And to You is the return". When the people recited it, their tongues became subdued with it. Then Allâh revealed: "The Messenger believes in what is sent down to him from His Lord, and so do the believers (following him). Each one believes in Allâh and His angels and His Books and His Messengers, saying: We differentiate not between any of His Messengers; and they say: We hear and seek your forgiveness, our Lord! And to You is the return". When they (the Companions) said the same, Allâh abrogated this verse and Allâh the All-Great, revealed a new one replacing it: "Allâh burdens not a soul beyond its capacity. It gets every good that it earns and it suffers every ill that it earns. Our Lord! Punish us not, if we forget or make a mistake". (When the Companions repeated the same words) Allâh said: Yes: (The Companions further repeated the words as revealed to Prophet Muhammad صلى الله عليه وسلم) Our Lord! Do not lay on us a burden as that you had laid on those before us. Allâh said: Yes. (The Companions further repeated) Our Lord! impose not on us (burdens) which we have no strength to bear. Allâh said: Yes. (The Companions further repeated) And pardon us and provide us protection; and have Mercy on us. You are our Patron, so please grant us victory over the disbelieving people". Allâh said: Yes. (2:285,6)

(This *Hadith* is sound and reported by Muslim).

The people of the Torah and Bible used to say to their Prophets (we hear and disobey). Unlike them the Companions of Prophet Muhammad صلى الله عليه وسلم were guided by him to say: "We hear and will obey, seek your forgiveness O Lord and to You is our return", so a true Muslim should be obedient to the commands of the Qur'ân and traditions of Prophet Muhammad صلى الله عليه وسلم .

****

(١٠٤) عَنْ عَائِشَةَ رَضِيَ اللهُ عَنْهَا أَنَّ رَسُولَ اللهِ ﷺ قَالَ: «مَا مِنْ يَوْمٍ أَكْثَرُ مِنْ أَنْ يُعْتِقَ اللهُ فِيهِ عَبْدًا مِنَ النَّارِ مِنْ يَوْمِ عَرَفَةَ، وَإِنَّهُ لَيَدْنُو ثُمَّ يُبَاهِي بِهِمُ الْمَلَائِكَةَ فَيَقُولُ: مَا أَرَادَ هَؤُلَاءِ».

«حديث صحيح لغيره» [رواه مسلم]

Superiority of the Day of 'Arafah when the Lord عز وجل becomes proud of the pilgrims

104) Narrated 'Aisha رضى الله عنها that Allâh's Messenger صلى الله عليه وسلم said: There is no day other than the day of 'Arafah when Allâh releases more of His slaves from Hell. Indeed, He draws near and proudly tells His angels about the pilgrims. Then He asks: What do these slaves of Mine seek? (so He forgives them).

(This *Hadîth* is sound and reported by Muslim).

****

(١٠٥) عَنْ جَابِرٍ رَضِيَ اللهُ عَنْهُ قَالَ: قَالَ رَسُولُ اللهِ ﷺ: «مَا مِنْ أَيَّامٍ عِنْدَ اللهِ أَفْضَلُ مِنْ عَشْرِ ذِي الحِجَّةِ، قَالَ فَقَالَ رَجُلٌ: يَارَسُولَ اللهِ هُنَّ أَفْضَلُ أَمْ عَدَدُهُنَّ جِهَادًا فِي سَبِيلِ اللهِ؟ قَالَ: هُنَّ أَفْضَلُ مِنْ عَدَدِهِنَّ جِهَادًا فِي سَبِيلِ اللهِ، وَمَا مِنْ يَوْمٍ

أَفْضَلُ عِنْدَ اللهِ مِنْ يَوْمِ عَرَفَةَ يَنْزِلُ اللهُ تَبَارَكَ وَتَعَالَى إِلَى السَّمَاءِ الدُّنْيَا فَيُبَاهِي بِأَهْلِ الأَرْضِ أَهْلَ السَّمَاءِ فَيَقُولُ انظُرُوا إِلَى عِبَادِي جَاءُوْا شُعْثًا غُبْرًا حَاجِّيْنَ جَاءُوْا مِنْ كُلِّ فَجٍّ عَمِيْقٍ يَرْجُوْنَ رَحْمَتِي وَلَمْ يَرَوْا عَذَابِي، فَلَمْ يُرَ يَوْمٌ أَكْثَرُ عَتِيْقًا مِنَ النَّارِ مِنْ يَوْمِ عَرَفَةَ». «حديث حسن لغيره» [زوائد ابن حبان]

105) Narrated Jabir رضى الله عنه: Allâh's Messenger صلى الله عليه وسلم said: No other days are better to Allâh than the first ten days of *Hajj* Month. The narrator said: A man asked: O Allâh's Messenger! Are these days better or the similar number of days of fighting in the cause of Allâh? The Prophet (صلى الله عليه وسلم) said: These days are better than the same number of days of fighting for the sake of Allâh . And no other day is better to Allâh than the day of 'Arafah when Allâh تبارك وتعالى descends to the lowest heaven (world's sky) and boasts of the people on earth to the inhabitants of heaven (angels) and says: Look at My slaves who have come with grown hair covered with dust to perform *Hajj*. They have come from all directions hoping for My mercy though they haven't seen My punishment. So there is no other day than the day of 'Arafah when the people are released abundantly from Fire.

(This *Hadîth* is considered sound by others, and reported by Ibn Hibban).

****

(١٠٦) عَنْ أَبِي هُرَيْرَةَ رَضِيَ اللهُ عَنْهُ قَالَ: قَالَ رَسُولُ اللهِ ﷺ: «قَالَ اللهُ: كُلُّ عَمَلِ ابْنِ آدَمَ لَهُ إِلاَّ الصِّيَامَ فَإِنَّهُ لِي وَأَنَا

أَجْزِى بِهِ وَالصِّيَامُ جُنَّةٌ، وَإِذَا كَانَ يَوْمُ صَوْمِ أَحَدِكُمْ فَلاَ يَرْفُثْ وَلا يَصْخَبْ فَإِنْ سَابَّهُ أَحَدٌ أَوْ قَاتَلَهُ فَلْيَقُلْ إِنِّي امْرُؤٌ صَائِمٌ، وَالَّذِي نَفْسُ مُحَمَّدٍ بِيَدِهِ لَخَلُوفُ فَمِ الصَّائِمِ أَطْيَبُ عِنْدَ اللهِ مِنْ رِيْحِ المِسْكِ لِلصَّائِمِ فَرْحَتَانِ يَفْرَحُهُمَا: إِذَا أَفْطَرَ فَرِحَ بِفِطْرِهِ وَإِذَا لَقِيَ رَبَّهُ فَرِحَ بِصَوْمِهِ». «حديث صحيح»

[رواه البخاري ومسلم]

Superiority of Fasting (*Saum*)

106) Narrated Abû Huraira رضى الله عنه: Allâh's Messenger صلى الله عليه وسلم said: Allâh said: Every good deed performed by son of Adam is a credit for him but fasting is exclusively Mine and I give reward for it. Fasting is a shield against sins. Therefore, when any of you is fasting he should neither indulge in obscene language nor raise the voice. If any one abuses him or quarrels with him, he should say: I am fasting. By Him in Whose Hand is Muhammad's soul! The smell coming out of the mouth of a person fasting is more pleasant to Allâh than the smell of musk. And he who fasts has two occasions of joy. One is when he breaks the fast, and the second is when he meets his Lord.

(This *Hadîth* is sound and reported by Bukhâri and Muslim).

****

(١٠٧) عَنْ أَبِي هُرَيْرَةَ رَضِيَ اللهُ عَنْهُ قَالَ: قَالَ رَسُولُ اللهِ ﷺ: «لَمَّا خَلَقَ اللهُ آدَمَ وَنَفَخَ فِيْهِ الرُّوْحَ عَطِسَ فَقَالَ الحَمْدُ للهِ

فَحَمِدَ اللهَ بِإِذْنِ اللهِ فَقَالَ لَهُ رَبُّهُ يَرْحَمُكَ رَبُّكَ يَاآدَمُ اذْهَبْ إِلَى أُولَئِكَ المَلاَئِكَةِ إِلَى مَلإٍ مِّنْهُمْ جُلُوسٌ فَسَلِّمْ عَلَيْهِمْ فَقَالَ: اَلسَّلاَمُ عَلَيْكُمْ فَقَالُوا: وَعَلَيْكَ السَّلاَمُ وَرَحْمَةُ اللهِ ثُمَّ رَجَعَ إِلَى رَبِّهِ فَقَالَ: هَذِهِ تَحِيَّتُكَ وَتَحِيَّةُ بَنِيكَ بَيْنَهُمْ، وَقَالَ اللهُ عَزَّ وَجَلَّ وَعَلاَ وَيَدَاهُ مَقْبُوضَتَانِ: اِخْتَرْ أَيَّهُمَا شِئْتَ فَقَالَ اخْتَرْتُ يَمِيْنَ رَبِّي وَكِلْتَا يَدَيْ رَبِّي يَمِيْنٌ مُبَارَكَةٌ ثُمَّ بَسَطَهَا فَإِذَا فِيْهَا آدَمُ وَذُرِّيَّتُهُ فَقَالَ: أَيْ رَبِّ مَا هَؤُلاَءِ؟ فَقَالَ: هَؤُلاَءِ ذُرِّيَّتُكَ فَإِذَا كُلُّ إِنْسَانٍ مَكْتُوبٌ عُمْرُهُ بَيْنَ عَيْنَيْهِ فَإِذَا فِيْهِمْ أَضْوَؤُهُمْ أَوْ مِنْ أَضْوَئِهِمْ لَمْ يُكْتَبْ لَهُ إِلاَّ أَرْبَعُوْنَ سَنَةً قَالَ يَارَبِّ مَا هَذَا؟ قَالَ: هَذَا ابْنُكَ دَاوُد وَقَدْ كُتِبَ لَهُ عُمْرُهُ أَرْبَعِيْنَ سَنَةً، قَالَ: أَي رَبِّ زِدْهُ فِي عُمْرِهِ. قَالَ: ذَاكَ الَّذِي كَتَبْتُ لَهُ قَالَ: فَإِنِّي جَعَلْتُ لَهُ مِنْ عُمْرِي سِتِّيْنَ سَنَةً، قَالَ: أَنْتَ وَذَاكَ اسْكُنِ الْجَنَّةَ فَسَكَنَ الْجَنَّةَ مَاشَاءَ اللهُ ثُمَّ أُهْبِطَ مِنْهَا، وَكَانَ آدَمُ يَعُدُّ لِنَفْسِهِ فَأَتَاهُ مَلَكُ المَوْتِ فَقَالَ لَهُ آدَمُ: قَدْ عَجِلْتَ قَدْ كُتِبَ لِي أَلْفُ سَنَةٍ قَالَ: بَلَى وَلَكِنَّكَ قَدْ جَعَلْتَ لاِبْنِكَ دَاوُدَ مِنْهَا سِتِّيْنَ سَنَةً فَجَحَدَ فَجَحَدَتْ ذُرِّيَّتُهُ وَنَسِيَ فَنَسِيَتْ ذُرِّيَّتُهُ فَمِنْ يَوْمَئِذٍ أُمِرَ بِالْكِتَابَةِ وَالشُّهُوْدِ». «حديث صحيح لغيره»

[ابن ابي عاصم وابن حبان في الزوائد والحاكم في المستدرك]

Origin of writing and making witnesses

107) Narrated Abû Huraira رضى الله عنه: Allâh's Messenger صلى الله عليه وسلم said: When Allâh created Adam and breathed soul into him, he sneezed. He said: Praise be to Allâh, by His permission. At this his Lord said to him: Your Lord has bestowed mercy on you. O Adam! Go to those angels sitting there and greet them. So Adam said: السلام عليكم (peace be upon you). They responded to him. On you too the same and Allâh's mercy (وعليكم السلام ورحمة الله). Then he came back to his Lord. Allâh said: It will be your greeting and the greeting of your offsprings. Allâh عزوجل said having made His Hands closed: Select any one of them. Adam said: I select the right hand and both the hands of my Lord are right and blessed. Then Allah spread it. There was Adam and his generation. Adam asked: O Lord! Who are these people? Allâh said: They are your children. Every human being's life is written between his eyes. Among them was a man with the brightest face. For him was written only forty years of age. Adam said: O Lord! Who is this fellow? Allâh said: This is your son Dâ'ud (David). His life span is written forty years. Adam said: O Lord! Increase his age. Allâh said: This is what I have written down for him. He said: Then I give him sixty years of my age. Allâh said: This is between you and him. Live in Paradise. He lived there as long as Allâh wished. Then he was descended from it to earth. Adam was counting his age. Then the death angel came to him. Adam said to him: You have come earlier. For me, one thousand years have been written. The angel said: Yes, but out of them you have given sixty years to your son Dâ'ud. Adam denied that so his successors also denied. He forgot, so his successors also forgot. From that day, Allah ordered writing down and making witnesses (for pledges).

(This *Hadîth* is sound and reported by Ibn Abi Asim,

Ibn Hibban and Hakim in his *Mustadrak*).

This *Hadith* teaches us that one should write down his debts, loans to others and his pledges, because he may die any minute or may get into conflict with the second party. Unless there are witnesses and something written, his rights will not be proved. This will affect his life as well as that of his heirs.

****

(١٠٨) عَنْ أَبِي هُرَيرَةَ رَضِيَ اللهُ عَنْهُ قَالَ: قَالَ رَسُولُ اللهِ ﷺ: «جَاءَ مَلَكُ الْمَوْتِ إِلَى مَوْسَى عَلَيْهِ السَّلاَمُ فَقَالَ لَهُ: أَجِبْ رَبَّكَ قَالَ فَلَطَمَ مُوْسَى عَلَيْهِ السَّلاَمُ عَيْنَ مَلَكِ الْمَوْتِ فَفَقَأَهَا قَالَ: فَرَجَعَ الْمَلَكُ إِلَى اللهِ تَعَالَى فَقَالَ: إِنَّكَ أَرْسَلْتَنِي إِلَى عَبْدٍ لَكَ لاَ يُرِيْدُ المَوْتَ وَقَدْ فَقَأَ عَيْنَيَّ قَالَ: فَرَدَّ اللهُ إِلَيْهِ عَيْنَهُ وَقَالَ: ارْجِعْ إِلَى عَبْدِي فَقُلْ اَلْحَيَاةَ تُرِيْدُ؟ فَإِنْ كُنْتَ تَرِيْدُ الْحَيَاةَ فَضَعْ يَدَكَ عَلَى مَتْنِ ثَوْرٍ فَمَا تَوَارَتْ يَدَكَ مِنْ شَعْرِهِ فَإِنَّكَ تَعِيْشُ بِهَا سَنَةً قَالَ: ثُمَّ مَهْ؟ قَالَ: ثُمَّ تَمُوْتُ قَالَ: فَالآنَ مِنْ قَرِيْبٍ رَبِّ أَمِتْنِي مِنَ الأَرْضِ المُقَدَّسَةِ رَمِيةً بِحَجَرٍ».

«حديث صحيح» [رواه مسلم]

The story of Mûsa and the Angel of Death

108) Narrated Abû Huraira رضى الله عنه: that Allâh's Messenger صلى الله عليه وسلم said: Once the Death Angel came to Mûsa (Moses) عليه السلام and said to him: Respond to the order of your Lord. The Prophet (صلى الله عليه وسلم) said: Mûsa عليه السلام hit the angel over his eye and gouged it out. The Prophet صلى الله عليه وسلم) added: The

angel returned to Allâh, the Exalted, and complained: You sent me to a slave who does not want death. Rather he has ganged out my eye. The Prophet (صلى الله عليه وسلم) said: Allâh set the angels eye right and said: Go back to My slave and ask him: Do you want life? If you wish to live long, put your hand on the back of an ox. The more hair you grasp in your hand, the more years you will live. At this Mûsa عليه السلام said: Then what will happen? The angel said: Then you have to die. Mûsa said: It is better to die now. Then he invoked Allâh: O Lord! Let me die near the Holy Land (Palestine) by a shot of a stone.

(This *Hadîth* is sound and reported by Muslim).

This *Hadith* highlights the fact that nobody wants to die or rather fears the idea. This fear of the inner-self teaches us another fact, namely, that people fear the unknown conditions of them in the Hereafter. Death is not the end. Innerselves believe that there is something after death, but the disbelievers reject this idea.

****

(١٠٩) عَنْ أَبِي هُرَيرَةَ رَضِيَ اللهُ عَنْهُ عَنِ النَّبِيِّ ﷺ قَالَ: «بَيْنَمَا أَيُّوبُ يَغْتَسِلُ عُرْيَانًا خَرَّ عَلَيْهِ رِجْلُ جَرَادٍ مِنْ ذَهَبٍ فَجَعَلَ يَحْثِي فِي ثَوْبِهِ فَنَادَى رَبُّهُ: يَاأَيُّوبُ أَلَمْ أَكُنْ أَغْنَيْتُكَ عَمَّا تَرَى؟ قَالَ: بَلَى يَارَبِّ وَلَكِنْ لاَغِنىً لِي عَنْ بَرَكَتِكَ».

«حديث صحيح» [رواه البخاري]

Allâh's Grace on His Prophet Ayub (Job) عليه السلام

109) Narrrated Abû Huraira رضى الله عنه: The Prophet صلى الله عليه وسلم said: While Ayub عليه السلام was naked, taking a bath, a swarm of gold locusts fell on him. He started collecting them in his garment. At this, his Lord said: O Ayub! Have

I not bestowed you with enough (wealth) to make you dispensable with what you see? He replied: Yes, my Lord! But I can't dispense with Your blessings.

(This *Hadîth* is sound and reported by Bukhâri).

****

(١١٠) عَنْ أُبَيِّ بْنِ كَعْبٍ رَضِيَ اللهُ عَنْهُ قَالَ: انْتَسَبَ رَجُلَانِ عَلَى عَهْدِ رَسُولِ اللهِ ﷺ فَقَالَ أَحَدُهُمَا أَنَا فُلَانُ بْنِ فُلَانٍ فَمَنْ أَنْتَ لاَ أُمَّ لَكَ فَقَالَ رَسُولُ اللهِ ﷺ: «انْتَسَبَ رَجُلَانِ عَلَى عَهْدِ مُوسَى عَلَيْهِ السَّلَامُ فَقَالَ أَحَدُهُمَا أَنَا فُلَانُ بْنُ فُلَانٍ حَتَّى عَدَّ تِسْعَةً فَمَنْ أَنْتَ لاَ أُمَّ لَكَ قَالَ: أَنَا فُلَانُ بْنُ فُلَانٍ ابْنُ الإِسْلَامِ. قَالَ: فَأَوْحَى اللهُ إِلَى مُوسَى عَلَيْهِ السَّلَامُ إِنَّ هَذَيْنِ الْمُنْتَسِبَيْنِ أَمَّا أَنْتَ أَيُّهَا الْمُنْتَمِيُ أَوِ الْمُنْتَسِبُ إِلَى تِسْعَةٍ فِي النَّارِ فَأَنْتَ عَاشِرُهُمْ، وَأَمَّا أَنْتَ يَا هَذَا الْمُنْتَسِبُ إِلَى اثْنَيْنِ فِي الْجَنَّةِ فَأَنْتَ ثَالِثُهُمَا فِي الْجَنَّةِ». «إسناده صحيح» [رواه مسند أحمد]

Hazardousness of claim to the Pre-Islâmic Period of Ignorance

110) Narrated Ubai bin Ka'b رضى الله عنه: During the lifetime of Allâh's Messenger صلى الله عليه وسلم, two men attributed their family lineage. One of them said: I am such and such son of such and such but who are you? You have no mother. Allâh's Messenger صلى الله عليه وسلم added: In the lifetime of Mûsa عليه السلام, two men attributed their lineage. One of them said: I am such and such son of such and such till he

counted nine. So who are you? You have no mother. The second said: I am such and such son of such and such son of Islâm. The Prophet صلى الله عليه وسلم said: Allâh revealed to Mûsa عليه السلام to address these attributers: As for you who attributed yourself to nine, they are all in Hell and you are the tenth. As for you who attributed yourself to two (and Islam), they are in Paradise and you are the third.

(This *Hadîth* is reported in *Musnad Ahmad* and its chain of authorities is sound.)

Islam recognizes only the righteous man regardless of his origin or race, wealth, or background. The more good deeds he performs the better he is among his fellows. On the same analogy the disobedient to Allah عز وجل , is the worst regardless of his colour or origin, wealth, rank or career etc.

****

Miguel 973-956-0157